FABULOUS

faux florals

FABULOUS
faux florals

ARDITH BEVERIDGE, AIFD

50 easy,
extraordinary
projects with
silk flowers and
permanent
botanicals

CREATIVE
PUBLISHING
international

CHANHASSEN, MINNESOTA

Copyright © 2004
Creative Publishing international, Inc.
18705 Lake Drive East
Chanhassen, Minnesota 55317
1-800-328-3895
www.creativepub.com

President/CEO: Michael Eleftheriou
Vice President/Publisher: Linda Ball
Vice President/Retail Sales: Kevin Haas

FABULOUS FAUX FLORALS

Executive Editor: Alison Brown Cerier
Managing Editor: Yen Le
Art Director/Designer: Lois Stanfield
Senior Editor: Linda Neubauer
Photo Stylist: Joanne Wawra
Director of Production & Photography: Kim Gerber
Photographer: John Abernathy
Color Specialist: Tate Carlson
Studio Services Manager: Jeanette Moss McCurdy
Contributors: Design Master, Koehler & Dramm Wholesale
Florists, Schuster of Texas, Smithers-Oasis

Library of Congress Cataloging-in-Publication Data

Beveridge, Ardith.
    Fabulous faux florals : 50 easy, extraordinary projects with
    silk flowers and permanent botanicals / Ardith Beveridge.
        p. cm.
    Includes index.
    ISBN 1-58923-132-5
    1. Silk flowers. 2. Silk flower arrangement. I. Title.

TT890.7B48 2004
745.92--dc22

                            2003067432

Printed by R.R. Donnelley:
10 9 8 7 6 5 4 3 2 1

Contents

ABOUT THE AUTHOR

Ardith Beveridge, AIFD, AAF, PFCI, *is a master floral designer, educator, and judge. She is the director of education and instructor for the Koehler & Dramm Institute of Floristry. She also co-owns a floral design video production company, Floral Communications Group Inc., and is the instructor in the company's twelve series of do-it-yourself videos. Ardith's creativity and enthusiasm have captivated audiences in programs and workshops across the country and internationally. By special invitation, Ardith has designed for presidential inaugurations and other prestigious national and international events. She also appears regularly on television.*

Her professional certifications include the American Institute of Floral Designers, American Academy of Floriculture, Professional Floral Communicators International, Society of Floristry LTD (England), and the Canadian Academy of Floral Arts. She is an endorsed design education specialist for Teleflora wire service and a master designer for FTD.

The Joys of Faux Florals

HAVE YOU EVER FOUND YOURSELF WONDERING whether or not a flower in an arrangement was real? Did you just *have* to touch it to find out? Then you know how realistic and gorgeous faux florals have become!

Faux florals—also known as silk flowers and permanent botanicals—have become very popular decorating accents. They are seen in more and more homes, complementing decorating styles from casual country to contemporary to elegant. Through their color, texture, and style, faux floral designs can bring a room to life. Of course, fresh flowers can do this as well, but you'll enjoy the faux flowers far longer.

Faux florals are also perfect seasonal accents. What would spring be without daffodils, summer without daisies and roses, fall without mums, winter without evergreens? When the season changes, store the design to enjoy next year.

In many ways, faux florals are easier to work with than fresh flowers. The wired stems are easy to manipulate and will hold the shape you give them. And the flowers won't wilt or break.

On the creative side, faux florals open up new possibilities for your designs. They're always in season. They're sold in many different forms. They also come in more colors than their natural counterparts; if you need a blue rose for an arrangement, you can find one.

On the most practical level of all, consider that faux florals never need watering, and won't make anyone sneeze!

So get ready to discover the joys of creating with faux florals. Here are fifty original floral designs for table pieces, wreaths, swags, topiaries, and baskets. All the materials and tools are readily available in hobby and craft stores. Some specialty items can be ordered through your local florist. I'll teach you everything you need to know. There are complete materials lists and step-by-step instructions, plus lots of photographs. You may think that some of the pieces look difficult, but I assure you that you can make each and every one of them, even if you are an absolute beginner.

There are several ways you can approach a project. If you love every aspect of the design and want to create it exactly as pictured, simply follow my directions. If you have difficulty finding a particular floral material, feel free to substitute something with similar color, shape, and texture, using the photos on pages 15 to 18 as a guide. If the shape and style are right but you need a different color, simply choose similar flowers in your own color scheme, using the information on color (pages 9 to 11) to help you.

I know you are eager to start creating floral arrangements—it's my passion, too—but before you begin, please read through the first section. You'll find valuable information on materials and techniques—the same information that I include when I teach floral design classes to crafters and budding professionals. Then pick your first project, and enjoy!

—*Ardith Beveridge*

Techniques
AND DESIGN

Creating fabulous floral designs is much easier than you might think, even for an absolute beginner. This book will tell you how, and this section will start you out right. In a short time, you'll learn some useful concepts of floral design (nothing technical); be introduced to the tools, materials, and florals; and get step-by-step instructions for techniques you will use again and again as you create with faux florals.

FLORAL DESIGN BASICS

WHENEVER you choose a design from this book, or make your own design, start by thinking about where you plan to put the finished piece. Perhaps you want a wonderful arrangement for a side table in your family room. Maybe you want a seasonal wreath to put over the fireplace or a fall centerpiece for your dining room table. A floral arrangement can brighten any area, from the entryway to the bathroom vanity, and can sit at any height, from the floor to an overhead ledge.

Location affects many aspects of good floral design. For example, it determines the angles from which the piece will be seen. A centerpiece has to look good from every seat at the table. In fact, many table arrangements are seen from the sides as well as the front. On the other hand, a vase on an entry table will probably not be seen from the back—unless, of course, it's in front of a mirror! An arrangement on a low coffee table will be seen from above. A wreath over a fireplace is often seen from the side and the bottom as well as the front. You want to pick a design that will look good from all the visible sides.

Location also affects how big the arrangement should be. Do you want a focal point for the room, or an accent? The design should fit the available space around and above it without being intrusive and should be similar in scale to the rest of the room's furnishings.

If people will walk closely by the arrangement, the flowers can't stick out. This becomes a consideration with many wall designs and with table designs that are placed in halls and entrances. Also consider whether the design will be in a formal or quiet space, or where children will be playing.

Will the arrangement be seasonal or year-round? Many people enjoy changing their faux florals with the seasons, mirroring the flowers that would be growing during that time. However, you may want to create something that will look appropriate longer. There are designs—called "trans-seasonal"—that can span at least two seasons, usually spring to summer or fall to winter. An evergreen design that doesn't scream

"Christmas" might be appropriate from the day after Thanksgiving through the end of the winter. Many designs can also be altered to extend their life by switching some or all of the flowers or adding accents associated with the season, such as fall foliage or a bird's nest.

Choosing and Combining Colors

Color is the most important element of any floral design. After all, color is what flowers are all about. It's the first thing people notice. When you look at the design below, the first thing you see is pink! Also, more than any other element of a design, color interacts with the surroundings. Obviously, every flower does not come in every color, so your choices are limited to what is available. There are endless ways to combine colors, and experimenting with color is lots of fun. Here are some insights that will help you choose and combine colors effectively.

First, floral designs usually look best when one color dominates and the other colors support it. A rule of thumb is to use two-thirds of the dominant color, a quarter of the second color, and about a tenth of an accent color. Dark, intense colors usually work best in the center or base of the design, with light colors toward the edges. However, you may want to mix a few darker flowers near the outside of the design and a few lighter colors near the center to help it all balance.

Warm colors (red, orange, yellow) tend to dominate other colors and may seem to project out from the design. Cool colors (green, blue, and violet) are calm and restful. They tend to blend into the background of a floral design.

Consider the ways the room's lighting will affect the colors. In dim light, colors look muted. The yellow glow of candlelight and incandescent lighting can turn pink to peach and baby blue to gray. Cool colors and blends tend to fade away in dim light.

Floral designers, like artists, use the color wheel to show the relationship between colors and to help them choose colors that will work well together. On a color wheel, the twelve basic colors are arranged by how they are created and how they relate to each other.

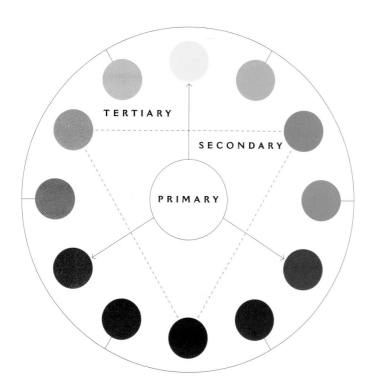

Red, yellow, and blue are called primary colors as they are not made from other colors. Orange, green, and violet are called secondary colors. Each is made by combining equal amounts of primary colors. Red plus yellow equals orange. Yellow plus blue equals green. Blue plus red equals violet. The

two-name colors (red-orange, blue-violet) are called tertiary. They are made by combining one primary color and one secondary color in equal or unequal amounts.

The color wheel can help you anticipate how certain combinations of colors will look in a floral design. Here are some of the possible color schemes for floral designs.

Monochromatic. This is a design in one color. The design will be more interesting if the color is used in various intensities. In the example below, pale yellow flowers are accented with bright yellows, which is more interesting than a design of all bright yellows. In monochromatic arrangements, textures become more important.

Analogous. An analogous design uses colors that are next to each other on the color wheel. For example, the design below uses various shades of violet, red-violet, and blue-violet.

Complementary. This scheme uses florals in colors located on opposite sides of the color wheel—for example, lime green cabbage leaves and fuchsia gerberas. The design will have strong contrast.

Triadic. This scheme uses colors that are the same distance apart on the color wheel. When used correctly, a triadic design can be rich and dramatic. The red, yellow, and blue flowers, used in the watering can arrangement below, form a triadic color scheme.

Split complementary. This scheme combines a main color with the two colors on either side of its complementary color. This enhances the main color and brings richness to the design. In the example below, red-violet and blue-violet are the split complements to yellow.

Shapes of Floral Designs

Asymmetrical design. A design in which each side has different colors, flowers, or other components, but both sides are equally important.

Crescent. A curved shape that narrows at each end.

Formal linear design. A design in which a few materials are carefully placed to emphasize their forms and lines.

Horizontal design. A scheme in which most of the lines of the design are parallel to the surface on which it is placed.

Oval. A flattened circle.

Parallel. An arrangement in which all the stems or groups of stems point in the same direction.

Round design. A design shaped like a circle or sphere.

Square. A design with four sides of equal length and four right angles.

Topiary. A design in which a slender stem or other materials support materials at the top.

Vertical design. A tall, narrow design that does not extend beyond the width of the container.

THE FLORALS

WHAT IS A "faux floral"? The word "faux" is French for "false." Faux florals are artificial flowers, but today's products are often so realistic that it's difficult to tell that they are not real. In the floral industry, faux florals are properly called "permanent botanicals." Though they are commonly referred to as "silk flowers," most are not made of silk but rather of polyester, latex, plastic, or a combination of materials.

Faux florals can be purchased in a wide range of qualities and prices from inexpensive stems in solid colors to realistic stems with shading and veining. Most are made by machine. Hand-wrapped florals, at the higher end, are assembled by hand, though the parts may be made by machine. They may be parchment or fabric and are very realistic with wired stems and leaves. Some parchment and fabric flowers are dipped in latex to make them look more natural. "Dried silk" flowers have a crinkled appearance with curled edges and resemble real dried flowers.

Faux florals are produced in four standard forms: the bush, the fantasy flower, botanical-like, and botanically correct.

Bush. A bush is a group of flowers and foliage on one stem, perhaps including accent flowers. A bush may include one type of flower or a combination. It is reasonably priced and easy to use whole or cut into individual stems.

Fantasy flowers. These flowers resemble real ones but have been designed to look different. For example, a flower might be made in a color in which it would not naturally exist, so that it can be used in a design where that color is needed.

Botanical-like. The florals are closer to the real thing, but the color, stem, foliage, or petal pattern has been changed to suit the desires of consumers. For example, a rose bush might have baby-blue flowers and have no dying flowers or broken stems.

Botanically correct. These are as close as possible to the real thing, though, of course, without the fragrance. The stem, pollen, leaf, root system, color, even branching structure are copied directly from nature. There is a remarkable degree of realism. Today's botanically correct florals look, feel, and are as flexible as real flowers. You may need to touch them to prove they are not fresh.

While botanically correct flowers and many botanical-like flowers are not inexpensive, they can be used as the focal point of an arrangement that includes inexpensive accent flowers. Top-quality florals are long lasting, so when you are tired of their first use, you can clean them and use them in other arrangements for added value.

Mosses

Sheet moss. A natural, dried moss, also called sphagnum moss, used to cover foam and other mechanics of a design. It is packaged in sheets or layers that can be separated as they are needed. Apply glue with a glue gun and attach small pieces of moss at a time. To give life and color to sheet moss, soak it in water, squeeze to remove excess moisture, and place it flat between newspapers or paper towels.

Spanish moss. A natural, soft gray, stringy dried moss used to cover foam and other mechanics, as well as to give a design an Old South or lodge look. Misting with water before use will soften it and cut down on dust.

Line flower →

Accent flower →

← *Form flower*

← *Mass flower*

Flower Roles

Flowers play certain roles in an arrangement, based on their shapes and sizes. If you can't find a particular flower, but you know its role, you can substitute something similar.

Line flower. Shaped like a spike or having a long stem, a line flower establishes the height and width of the arrangement. Examples are tuberose (shown), gladiolus, larkspur, and cattails.

Mass flower. A mass flower is a single, large, round flower that adds bulk and texture to a design. Examples are peonies (shown), hydrangea, carnations, and pincushion protea.

Form flower. A form flower has a distinctive shape that attracts the eye and gives interesting visual texture to the arrangement. Examples are lilies (shown) and irises.

Accent flower. Like the cineraria shown above, this flower accents the spaces between the main flowers in a design. Also called "filler flowers," they are usually added last, to fill empty spaces.

Line flowers

*Clockwise from left: tuberose, leper lily,
stock, gladiolus, lamium, snapdragon*

Mass flowers

Clockwise from left: anemone, peony, geranium, rose, hydrangea, ranunculus, dahlia

Form flowers

*Clockwise from left: bird-of-
paradise, lisianthus, alstroemeria,
iris, cockscomb, Gloriosa lily, lily*

Accent flowers

*Clockwise from left:
cineraria, wax flower,
Queen Anne's lace, wax
flower with grass, crassula,
miniature daisies, caspia*

CONTAINERS

A CONTAINER is a receptacle of any shape into which floral material is placed. The choices are countless and many are surprisingly inexpensive. The container is an important element of a design and often its inspiration. Perhaps you have an interesting vase or even a family heirloom. The right floral design can make it a focal point of the room.

The containers for the projects in this book were chosen carefully to complement the designs. You may be able to find a container that's quite similar, but you can also substitute something with the same general feel, style, and size.

When selecting a container, first consider the color. The color is often chosen to coordinate with the room's décor. The color can help the container become part of the design, too. Consider the shape—it needs to complement the design. The size matters, too. The container must be large enough to hold all materials comfortably. It should be not only physically large enough, but visually large enough for the design. Visualize the completed design in the container, in the space, in the room with its furniture. Finally, when you pick a container, think about the texture. The texture should make sense with the flowers as well as the room. For example, a basket or wooden box would be a good choice for a garden-style arrangement for a porch or sunroom. Another approach is to choose a contrasting texture; for example, if the room has many heavy, rough textures, an arrangement in a shiny, smooth container can become a focal point.

The size of a clay pot (for example, a 3-inch pot) is its inside diameter across the top. Measure inside the pot's surface from side to side.

Containers

Vases. Vases come in many sizes and shapes. They are made of glass, ceramic, plastic, and metal. A bud vase is small and holds a single stem. If it costs more than fifty dollars, you can pronounce it "voz"!

Ceramic. Ceramic containers come in a wide variety of sizes, shapes, and qualities. Choose one that is suitable for the occasion or the area in which it will be placed.

Baskets. Baskets come in a wide variety of sizes, shapes, and colors with and without handles, with and without liners and at every price. Baskets can be painted or stained to suit the design.

Utility containers. These are plain, inexpensive containers used when the container will not be visible or important. Perhaps the container will be used as a liner in a basket or will be wrapped with leaves or fabric.

Terra-cotta pots and containers (and plastic look-alikes). These are popular for garden designs. If the material is terra cotta, glue felt on the bottom of the pot to keep it from scratching a table.

Metal containers. Galvanized, rusted, silver, brass—lots of variety here.

MATERIALS AND TOOLS

Anchoring Materials

Styrofoam (1). Plastic foam with a hard or rough surface and sold in white, greens, and browns in various sizes and in shapes like hearts, squares, orbs, cones, wreaths, and crosses. It is used for thick-stemmed florals and materials on picks. When cutting Styrofoam with a knife, run the sharp blade edge into the side of an old candle before each cut, to help the knife cut smoothly and make less noise.

Dried floral foam (2). Sold in blocks, sheets, wreaths, and shapes and available in greens, browns, and brights. It grips stems securely and will not melt when glue or paint is applied.

Container weights (3). Marbles, sea glass, stones, and rocks, in a variety of colors, sizes, and shapes, used to add physical and visual weight to the design.

Floral plant foil (4). Pliable, colored, aluminum foil with a coating of plastic on both sides, used for fresh floral designs to protect from moisture. For faux floral design, it is used to keep foam particles from filtering through baskets.

Chicken wire (5). Wire net meshing in gray or green, used to provide stability in large designs.

Anchor pins (6). Small plastic circles with prongs. The circle is secured to the bottom of a container and the prongs hold floral foam in place.

Adhesives and Securing Materials

Glue pan (1). A small electric skillet (not deep-fat fryer) used to melt glue pellets.

Pan glue pellets (2). Nuggets or blocks of adhesive melted in a glue pan. Don't mix with glue sticks. Do not mix glues from different companies, as the chemical composition is different and the mixture may not adhere.

Paintbrush and honeystick (3). An inexpensive 2-inch paintbrush or a honeystick (page 25) used to apply glue to items too large or awkward to dip in the pan.

Small clay saucer (4). Placed in the glue pan to keep the brush and honeystick from resting on the bottom of the pan where they could burn.

Duct tape (5). One sided, all-purpose tape, 2" (5 cm) wide, with a silver-gray surface on one side. Used to attach foam temporarily.

Anchor tape (6). Narrow tape on a roll in green, white, or clear; 1/2" (1.3 cm) width for large projects and 1/4" (6 mm) width for small designs. Used for securing foam to the vessel.

Glue gun (7). Hot-glue tool used to secure foam and add trims. The high-temperature variety is best for faux floral work.

Glue sticks (8). For the glue gun; in white, clear, and glittered. This glue does not hold in cold temperatures, so don't use it on outdoor holiday

designs. Choose the type recommended by the manufacturer of your glue gun.

Floral tape (9). Self-sealing, wrapping tape in greens, browns, white, and rainbow colors. Used in floral design to wrap wires and lengthen stems.

Double-sided tape (10). Tape with adhesive on both sides; resists moisture and temperature extremes. Used for securing foam, candles, and accessory items like moss rocks.

Wood picks (11). Thin pieces of wood with a point on one end and a thin wire on the other, in green, brown, and natural. Used to secure objects like artificial fruit, to stabilize tall designs, and to extend stems. The 6" and 9" (15 and 23 cm) lengths will fill most of your needs.

Floral wire (12). Used to bind floral materials together and to lengthen stems that are too short for the design. Wires are 18" (46 cm) long and are sized in gauges from 16 to 28; the smaller the number, the thicker the wire. Wire in 24-gauge is versatile for faux floral designs.

Tools

Knife (1). Large, sharp knife for cutting foam and a smaller sharp knife for shaping foam. Choose a knife that feels comfortable in your hand. Sharpen after each use, and keep in a toolbox or other safe place.

Scissors (2). For cutting ribbon, foliage, fabrics, paper, or other items that do not contain metal. Sharpen regularly.

Shears (3). Very useful tool for cutting small wires and wired ribbon. Does not need to be sharpened.

Wire cutters (4). To cut faux floral stems. Blades are shaped for cutting close to the stem.

Utility snips (5). To cut thick stems, branches, thick wire, and chicken wire.

Awl (6). Sharp pointed metal rod for poking holes in firm materials.

Tape measure (7). For measuring foam size, stem lengths, and design proportions.

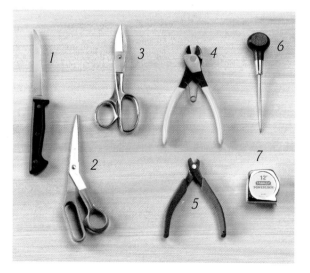

TECHNIQUES

Preparing Florals

When you buy a faux flower, it has been traveling a long way over a long time. It's been in a small box packed tightly with lots of other florals. So before you put it into a design, you need to fluff every flower and leaf. Bend and shape the stem. Open up the flowers and arrange the leaves in a natural way.

Many floral materials also need to be reinforced so that the flower heads won't separate from the stems later. This is particularly true when the head and leaves have been made separately and slipped over the stem. Check the flower parts. If they aren't securely fastened, remove those parts. Apply glue to the peg on the stem and put back the leaf or flowers. Allow the glue to dry before you work with the material. If you take this step, you'll save yourself frustration down the road.

Faux evergreens need to be opened and loosened before you start to design with them. Put on hand lotion and a pair of garden or light work gloves to protect your hands. Twist each stem a couple of times.

Cutting Stems

Always cut a floral stem at a sharp angle. The point makes it easier to insert the stem into foam. When the instructions say to cut a certain number of inches from the stem, that always means from the bottom of the original, main stem. Cut floral stems with a wire cutter.

Often a faux floral stem includes several flowers as well as foliage. The instructions may say to cut the stem into pieces. Find a section in the main stem that has a long distance between smaller branches. Cut the main stem at an angle just above the lower branch, as in the photo below. This will give the upper stem the length it needs. The flower at the end of the lower stem will top the newly cut stem.

If it is necessary to disguise the cut, touch up the area with paint to match the stem color. Often leaves can be bent or turned to hide a cut.

Cutting and Attaching Foam

1   Measure the opening of the container: side to side, front to back. Using a knife, cut the foam to fit the container. After making this rough cut, gently scrape a scrap of foam against the fitted piece to shape and smooth it.

2   Measure the height. This may be the same as the container depth or above or below the lip—check the instructions for the project. Place the foam into the container and mark where to cut with a marker. Remove and trim.

3   Dip the bottom of the foam into the glue pan. Place the foam into the container and press with your palm for a few seconds.

Attaching Foam with the Temporary Method

If you want to reuse a container, you can attach the foam temporarily rather than glue it.

1   Clean the inside of the container with white distilled vinegar to remove any film or oil.

2   Adhere duct tape over the bottom of the container.

3   Place the foam with the glue on it on the duct tape. This will secure it properly. When you want to reuse the container, pull off the duct tape and clean the container with soap and water.

Preparing Tall Containers

A tall table or floor design needs extra weight at the bottom for stability. Also, filling the entire container with foam would take a lot of foam!

Here's what to do. Place a heavy-duty garbage bag in the container. Put rocks, stones, clay pot pieces, or brick pieces into the bag. Then crumple newspaper and pack it into the container on top of the rocks. When you are 4" to 6" (10 to 15 cm) from the top, cut a piece of floral foam and secure it into the top, gluing it to the sides of the container if necessary. Depending on the design, the top of the floral foam may be even with the lip of the container or 2" to 4" (5 to 10 cm) above it.

Cut a piece of green chicken wire 2" (5 cm) bigger than the foam. Wrap the chicken wire around the floral foam and down into the container, pushing the open ends into the foam or container. Place a piece of green anchor tape across the top; secure it to the sides and trim off the excess.

Securing Foam to a Basket

This method allows you to reuse the basket later. It also prevents bits of foam from shedding out of the bottom of the basket.

1   Cut green plant foil to fit the bottom of the basket. Place in the basket.

2   Measure and cut the foam. Put the foam on top of the foil.

3   Remove the wire from the end of a wood pick. Place the pointed end into an opening on the outside of the basket. Insert the pick slowly into the basket, then into the foam. Stop when the squared end of the pick is still outside the basket. Repeat on all four sides.

4   Cover the exposed wood pick with a touch of hot glue and a touch of moss, leaves, branches, or flower heads.

Working with Styrofoam

Here are some tips for working with hard foams like Styrofoam.

Before you cut the foam, sketch the desired shape. You can cut with a sharp knife or a saw. Make sure you cut with the sharp edge directed away from your body. To remove loose particles, rub the pieces together.

When you glue foam, you can hold it in place while it's drying by inserting wire or picks. A cautionary note: Do not expose foam to flames or intense heat during storage, design, or final use.

Using a Glue Pan

A glue pan works at a lower and more variable temperature than a glue gun. Place the pan on a piece of hard plastic to protect your work surface. When you turn off the glue pan, you can keep the glue in it until next time. Set the temperature so that the glue is liquid but not smoking. There are two ways to apply the glue to materials.

Dipping. Floral foam and faux floral stems can be dipped into the glue pan before you secure them.

Brushing. When an object is too large or awkward to dip, you can transfer glue from the pan with a 2" (5 cm) paintbrush or a homemade honeystick. To make a honeystick, wrap a 12" (30.5 cm) chenille stem or pipe cleaner (one without metallics) around 2" (5 cm) at the end of a 9" (23 cm) wood pick or any strong natural wood stick or branch (nothing plastic, cloth, or metal).

Inserting Stems

1 Hold the stem in the place, at the height, and at the angle you think you'd like it. Move it around to be sure that this is where you want it.

2 Push the stem into the spot you've chosen to the right depth. Put a finger on the stem at the place where it leaves the foam, and keep the finger there as you pull out the stem. Mark the spot with a marker that is close in color to the stem, or with anchor tape that you can later remove.

3 Measure 2" to 3" (5 to 7.5 cm) below the mark. At this place, cut the stem at a sharp angle with a wire cutter. The point will pierce the foam, then as the stem gets larger, it will grip the foam securely.

4 Trim away any foliage or flowers that are in the 2" to 3" (5 to 7.5 cm) above the cut.

5 Place the stem into the desired place to check it once more before gluing. (As you gain experience, you will be able to skip this step.)

6 Dip the end of the stem into the glue pan. Immediately place the stem into the hole and hold it in place for a few seconds.

Using a Glue Gun

A glue gun is the best way to apply glue directly to a design—for example, to attach flowers or add trim. Heat the gun, place the tip where you want the glue, pull the trigger, and move the gun in a circular motion ending with an upward movement to break off the glue. The glue will be hot; if you aren't careful, you can get a nasty burn. Also, when the glue is hot it will ooze out of the gun end at a touch of the trigger, so please be careful.

Lengthening a Stem

There will be times when you need to lengthen a stem so that it will work in your design. Perhaps you've cut a stem apart into pieces, and some of the pieces just aren't long enough. You can easily extend a stem with wire.

1   Cut a floral wire as long as the present stem plus the length you want the stem to be extended. Hold the wire alongside the faux floral stem.

2   Wrap floral tape around the calyx (base of the blossom), gently stretching the tape and pressing the tape onto itself. Floral tape is a reversible strip of crepe paper coated with wax on either side. As the tape stretches, the wax is released to secure the floral tape to the stem. The warmth of your fingers softens the wax, causing the tape to stick to itself.

3   Twirl the floral stem with one hand, so the tape spirals around and down the stem, covering the stem and wire together. Stretch and warm the tape between the thumb and index finger of the other hand. The tape should overlap slightly with each wrap and leave no gaps. However, too much tape will give a bulky, unnatural appearance.

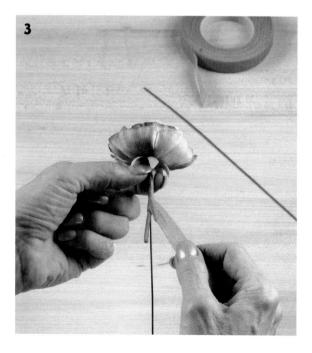

4   When you run out of floral stem, continue wrapping to the bottom of the wire. Then tear the tape from the roll (it is not necessary to cut it). Seal the end of the tape to the end of the wire by rolling the stem in your fingers.

Wrapping Floral Wire

Floral wire is often wrapped with tape to make it easier to handle and less visible in the design.

1   Hold the end of the tape at the top of the wire. Twirl the wire in one hand while you wrap it with tape in spirals moving down the wire. Overlap the tape slightly and leave no gaps.

2   At the bottom of the wire, tear the tape. Seal the tape to the end of the wire by rolling the wire between your fingers.

Dividing a Purchased Wreath

When you buy a grapevine or honeysuckle vine wreath as a base for an arrangement, you can embellish it with floral materials just the way it is, but you can also separate it into two or three less dense wreaths and get more for your money! You can form the vines into wreaths of different sizes. You can even divide a grapevine wreath and a honeysuckle vine wreath and combine pieces of each to make several wreath bases that have interesting texture. Here's how to separate and work with vines. You may want to use a pair of light garden gloves when separating and working with the vines.

1   Wrap ten 18" (46 cm), 26-gauge wires with brown floral tape, following the method used for wrapping wire above. Cut each of the taped wires into four parts. Place them in a vase or shallow container so they are easy to locate on the work table. (They are the same color as the vine and could be swept away with loose branches.)

2   Remove the vine that holds the wreath together. It is usually a larger vine that is wrapped around the entire wreath to secure and shape the

enclosed vines. Set this aside. Don't worry if it breaks; you can still use it.

3 Gently separate the wreath coil. Separate the vine into the amount and sizes of wreaths you have decided to make.

4 Gather two vine pieces in your hand. Wrap a piece of the taped wire around the two vines; twist the wire tight against the vines. Leave the wire ends long so you will be able to add more vines later. Always secure only two vines together at a time; more that that will slip and not hold securely.

5 Repeat step four in several places to establish the size and shape of the wreath. Then add more vines to the wreath, twisting the existing wire tails around them to hold them in place. Continue until the wreath is as dense as you want it.

6 Coil the wire ends around a pencil to resemble natural vine tendrils.

Hanging a Wall Design

Prepare a wreath or swag base for hanging before you make the floral design.

A table-top easel, purchased at an art supply store, works well for hanging your wreath or other wall design while you are working on it.

1 Hold the wreath or swag base where you'd like it to hang. Tie a small piece of ribbon at the center of the design. If the design is large or long, you may want to attach hangers in two places.

2 Wrap a 10" (25.5 cm) piece of 22-gauge wire with floral tape in a color that matches the design, following the method explained on page 26. For a large item, you may need a heavier wire.

3 Bend the wire into a U shape. At the ribbon marker, run the ends through the base from front to back, catching two or more large vines near the inner edge of a wreath or near the lower edge of a swag.

4 Twist the last 1" (2.5 cm) of the two wire ends together tightly.

5 Maneuver the twisted ends to the front so the U is on the back. Pull the U tight and twist the wire at the spot where it is touching the wall hanging. You will have a loop in your finger large enough to place on a nail or wall hanger.

6 Hide the twisted ends in the vines. Mark the hanger with the ribbon. This will help you design the wall hanging in the right position and find the hanger when you are finished and are ready to put the piece on your wall.

Making a Bow

Many ribbons are one-sided. The following method for making a loop bow keeps the decorative (right) side of the ribbon facing outward and the matte side hidden inside the loops.

1   Cut a 24-gauge wire in half and set it aside on the work table. Unroll about a yard (meter) of 1" (2.5 cm) wide ribbon, but don't cut it. Grasp the ribbon between your left thumb and index finger, with the right side (shiny side) of the ribbon facing up; leave a tail of the desired length below your hand.

2   Make a sharp half twist in the ribbon at the point where you are grasping it, and hold the twist between your thumb and finger; the matte side of the ribbon will now be facing up above your hand.

3   Bring the ribbon down over your thumb in a small loop, wrapping the ribbon flat against the twist on the underside; slip it between your thumb and finger. The matte side will again be facing up above your hand.

4   Make a sharp half twist in the ribbon again at the point where you are grasping it, and hold the twist between your thumb and finger. The right side of the ribbon will now be facing up above your hand.

5   Turn under the ribbon, forming a loop above your hand and bringing the matte side of the ribbon flat against the twists on the underside. Slip the ribbon between your thumb and finger. The matte side of the ribbon will now be facing up below your hand.

6   Make a sharp half twist in the ribbon again at the point where you are grasping it, and hold the twist between your thumb and finger. The right side of the ribbon will now be facing up below your hand.

7   Turn under the ribbon, forming an equal loop below your hand, bringing the matte side of the ribbon flat against the twists on the underside; slip it between your thumb and finger. The matte side will now be facing up above your hand.

8   Repeat steps 4 to 7 at least twice or until you have made the desired number of loops. Make each pair of loops the same size or slightly larger than the pair above them.

9   Give the ribbon a final half twist and slip the twist between your finger and thumb with the other twists. Cut the ribbon at an angle, leaving a tail of the desired length.

10   Insert a wire through the thumb loop so the middle of the wire rests under your thumb

and the end comes out between your index and middle finger.

11   Bend the wire ends down so they are parallel to each other and perpendicular to the back of the bow. Press the top of your right index finger tight against the underside of the bow between the wires. Holding the wires with the other fingers and palm of your right hand, remove your left thumb and index finger.

12   Grasp the bow loops with your left hand and turn them twice, so that the wires twist tightly between your right index finger and the bow back. Release the loops and give them a fluff.

Checking and Adjusting Your Arrangement

When you have completed your design, step back and look it over. Here are some things to check.

Are the flowers where you want them? Some may have been pushed out of place while you were designing. Each flower deserves its own space. Gently move the main flowers if they are touching one another.

Is there any paper still on the flowers? Check to be sure that the price tags and the information tags have been removed from the stems.

If you have cut stems, is the cut concealed? Is the foam covered?

Do you see any glue or glue strings? Set a hair dryer on hot, and run the air slowly over the design to melt away any glue strings.

Is the bottom of the arrangement clean and free of moss and glue?

Does the arrangement seem to flow together? Are you happy?

CLEANING AND STORING FLORALS

OVER TIME, faux florals can get dusty. You have several options for cleaning them.

First, there are several good sprays for cleaning faux flowers and foliage. Follow the directions on the package for the best results.

If the stems are not in a design, you can also clean them with soap and water. Put warm water and dish soap in a sink or bowl. Have another sink or bowl with water for rinsing. Test one stem first to see how it reacts to the water. Some lose their color; if this happens, use the spray product instead. If not, swish the stem in the water, then in the rinse water. Lay the stems on a cloth and let dry, or blow-dry with a hair dryer on the low, cool setting.

A third option is to take your flowers or finished design outside or into a garage and blow the dust away with a hair dryer.

To store a seasonal design, first place it in a large, dark, plastic bag. That way, the flowers will keep their color.

You'll also want to store the leftovers from your project. You can separate the florals by type, color, or season. Clear plastic, stackable storage boxes work very well. You can see what's inside, and the boxes take up little room. List what's in each container, and label the container for easy access. Today's leftovers are tomorrow's masterpieces, but only if they're in good shape and you know where they are.

10

12

Single Flower

TABLE DESIGNS

Designs with a single type of flower are among the easiest to make, yet they can be stunning. A simple vase design can be wonderful, but there are also many other ways to set off one or more stems of a flower. You can surround flowers with a bamboo armature, plant them in wheat grass, or encircle them with wreaths. Many of these designs can also be made with different florals to complement your home décor or the season of the year.

Singles in Silver

GROUPING INDIVIDUAL STEMS

This is a grouping of similar, small vases, each holding a single flower or stem. The group should have something in common—flowers in one color or one type, containers made of the same material, all herbs, all foliage—to create a sense of "family."

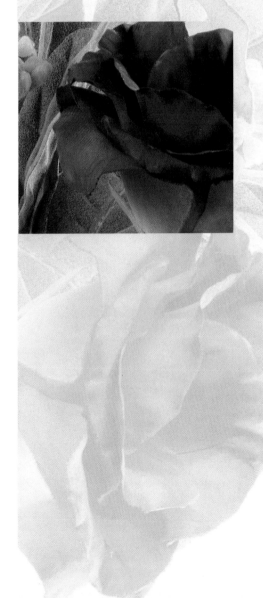

Singles in Silver

Florals

Single flowers or foliage stems, one for each container

Tools and materials

Three or more similar vases or other small containers (silvered, metal, glass, etc.)

Wire cutter

Dry floral foam

Knife

1   Place the chosen containers on your work surface. Arrange them in a straight line, a serpentine line, in a circle, or on a decorative tray. You can also put them along a table runner. If you are making a cluster, place taller vases closer to the center. Experiment until you feel a sense of balance and rhythm.

2   Place the flowers and foliage stems next to the vases and match them up. Think about which shape and size of flower will look best with each container. Try out a few options until you are pleased. You can always change your mind.

3 When you're satisfied with the choices, if the flower and vase are small, simply place the flower in the container. If the flower and container are large, or the flower needs support, cut foam so it will fill the container completely from side to side and sit 1" (2.5 cm) below the lip. Secure the foam into the container. Then insert the flower.

4 Look over the design and rearrange or change as you like.

VARIATION

There are many ways to arrange a grouping. Here, the same vases are in a circle. Starting at the yellow rose, the height increases as you move counter-clockwise, then dips before the circle starts again. The mirror holds the grouping together. This would be a great centerpiece.

MORE VARIATIONS

Same containers, but this time with white flowers—an elegant look. The possibilities for grouping single flowers are endless. Select red, white, and blue flowers and put a flag in one container for the Fourth of July. For fall, use field grasses, autumn florals, and a small gourd. At Easter, put a small colored egg in one of the containers.

Spring Lawn

CHANGING WITH THE SEASONS

This design brings spring indoors to your table. In a base of wheat grass, you "plant" faux versions of the small flowers that are growing outside at the time. For example, you might start with miniature daffodils in early spring, switch to lilies of the valley in May, and finish with gerberas in early summer. You can make one for a centerpiece, or several for a longer table or mantle.

Spring Lawn

Florals

Two 4" (10 cm) squares artificial wheat grass

One bush narcissus and grass

Two bushes lily of the valley

Six stems mini gerberas

Tools and materials

Oblong container

Dry floral foam

Knife

Glue pan and glue

Wire cutter

Plastic storage bags

1   Cut the foam so it will fill the container completely from side to side and sit 1" (2.5 cm) below the lip. Secure it to the container.

2   With the wire cutter, cut the base of the wheat grass to fit the entire container, covering the foam completely.

3   In early spring, cut at an angle the flower stems from the narcissus bush to various lengths. Insert the stems through the wheat grass into the foam, without gluing in place. Arrange naturally, not in a pattern.

4   In mid-spring, remove and clean the narcissus. Place them in a plastic zipper bag for reuse; label and store them. Cut at an angle the stems from the lily of the valley bushes. Place at random in

small patches of flowers and foliage, as they would grow by the porch of Grandma's house.

5 In late spring, remove the lily of the valley stems; clean and store as in step 4. Cut at an angle the gerbera stems at various lengths. Place at random.

Simply Stocks

THE SINGLE-FLOWER VASE

Bouquets of a single type of
flower are very popular. Choose
long-stemmed florals like roses,
peonies, or snapdragons. In this
design, coiled willows support
a bouquet of stock stems. This
approach, in which natural-
looking elements serve as the
support structure, is called hana-
kubari, which means "flower
holder" in Japanese.

Simply Stocks

Florals

Three branches faux curly willow

Nine stems stock with foliage

Tools and materials

Clear glass vase

Wire cutter

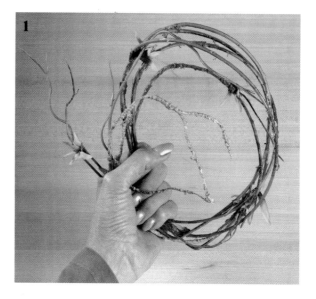

1 Shape and twist the willow branches by wrapping them around your hand.

2 Place them into the vase and arrange the branches to make a winding, irregular pattern. Curve a couple of branches down over the outside of the vase.

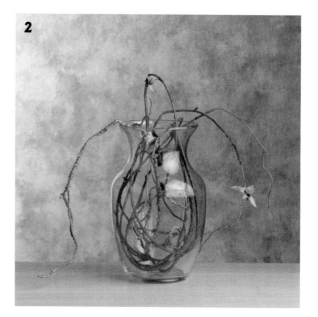

4

3 Cut some of the foliage from the main stems of stock, and set aside.

4 Place the first stem of stock on the right side of the vase with the head at 2 o'clock. Place the second on the left side with the head at 10 o'clock. Rotate the vase a half turn and repeat with the third and fourth stems. The stems will cross in the center of the vase and pass through the willow branches. Place the fifth stem of stock in the center, and the last four between the stems at the edges and the center, at lesser angles. You will have three levels of flowers.

5 Add the reserved foliage to fill in any gaps between the flowers above the glass vase.

6 Look over the design and make any necessary adjustments.

Lucky Bamboo

SIMULATED WATER

Lucky bamboo, also known as pencil bamboo, is said to bring prosperity and a full life. This faux bamboo looks real because it is set in simulated water. If you use this product, choose a floral with a plastic stem, and test for colorfastness by placing pieces of the stem in real water for two days. Because simulated water is permanent, you won't be able to reuse the vase or the flowers.

Lucky Bamboo

Florals

Five or six stems lucky bamboo with root system

Tools and materials

Clear glass vase

White distilled vinegar; cotton balls

Stones, river rock, marbles, or sea glass

Clear anchor tape

Scissors

Simulated water

Glass measuring cup for mixing simulated water (not reusable)

1   Fill the container with regular tap water to the level you like, to determine how much simulated water you will need to make. Make allowances for the space that will be taken up by the rocks and stems. Then measure how many cups of water will be needed, and write it down.

2   Wash and dry the vase thoroughly, inside and out. Allow the rocks and stems to dry, too. If any moisture at all is present, simulated water will not set. Put a few drops of vinegar on a cotton ball and rub around the lip of the vase to remove any traces of oil so the tape will stick.

3   Place your choice of stones, marbles, or other materials in the container a few at a time, to the height you want. Be careful not to shatter the glass.

4   Place the stems of the bamboo in the container in and around the stones.

4

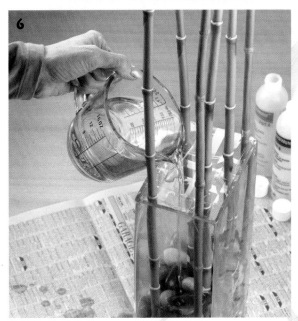

5 With the tape, form a grid across the container top to hold the stems securely in place. Leave an opening near the center so you can pour in the simulated water.

6 Mix the estimated amount of simulated water, following the package directions. Pour the two liquids down the sides of the measuring cup to avoid forming air bubbles—note that one will be thicker and will pour more slowly. Stir slowly for three to five minutes. Pour the liquid into the vase through the center opening, forming as few bubbles as possible.

7 Allow to cure for eight hours. Dispose of the measuring cup. Do not pour excess simulated water down a drain. Remove the tape. Clean the top and sides of the vase. Shape the stems for a natural look.

VARIATION
These callas came with realistic root structures that are included in this naturalistic design. Before the simulated water was added, pebbles and artificial soil mix were put in the bottom of the container. White glue was mixed with the "soil" to moisten it and keep it in place.

Asian Orchid

FAUX ORCHIDS

For a long time, orchid designs were exclusively upscale, but now these spectacular flowers are also seen in informal and natural arrangements. In this design, a rustic planter and willows create a casual setting with lots of movement. Faux orchids are available in many naturalistic colors and combinations and in many sizes and varieties. They look amazingly real!

Asian Orchid

Florals

Two Dendrobium orchid plants with root system

Nine branches fresh or dried curly willow, 2 ft. to 3 ft. (0.63 to 0.92 m) long

Sheet moss

Tools and materials

Container

Dry floral foam

Knife

Glue pan and glue

Wire cutter

1 Cut the foam so it will fill the container completely from side to side and sit 1" (2.5 cm) below the lip. Secure it into the container.

2 Cut 2" (5 cm) off the bottom of each orchid stem. Imagine the container divided into three parts from side to side. Insert one orchid stem one-third of the the distance from each side.

3 Cover the foam with moss.

4 Insert all the willow branches near the rim of the container, all the way around.

5 Look over the design and make any necessary adjustments.

Framed Callas

ENCIRCLING WITH WREATHS

This striking, contemporary design features two wreaths and a garland that circle the vase and frame the flowers. Choose wreaths and/or garlands with different textures, including evergreens for winter themes. This design calls for flowers with strong stems and bold color. These orange callas are perfect. Bands of colored ribbon carry the color throughout the design.

Framed Callas

Florals

Twelve callas, 24" (61 cm) long

Green-colored grapevine wreath, 16" (40.5 cm) diameter, with its opening slightly wider than the top of the vase

Four green wood hyacinth stakes, 14" (35.5 cm) long

Dried spiral birch wreath, 10" (25.5 cm) diameter

Faux eucalyptus garland, 6 ft. (1.85 m) long

Tools and materials

Tall, tapered (wider at the top), clear glass vase

1 yd. (0.92 m) ribbon in the same colors as the flowers

Scissors

Glue gun and glue

1 Insert two hyacinth stakes through the upper layer of the grapevine wreath, from side to side, about 2" (5 cm) apart. Insert the other two stakes across the wreath from front to back weaving them over and under the first stakes. Place the wreath on top of the vase so the stakes rest on top and the wreath hangs over the side.

2 Place the spiral birch wreath on top of the grapevine wreath. Circle the eucalyptus garland between the two wreaths.

3 Lay the callas on the work surface in pairs. Cut the ribbon into nine pieces, 3" (7.5 cm) long. Lay the ribbon pieces on the stems at varied heights so there will be color in the vase and above the wreaths. Touch a calla stem with glue, wrap the ribbon tightly around the pair, secure again with glue. Repeat with each pair of callas.

4 Gently place each pair of callas into the vase, varying the height of the ribbon bands to lead the eye in and around the design.

5 Look over the design and make any necessary adjustments.

Irises in River Cane

ARMATURES FOR FLOWERS

In this garden design, the irises seem to grow right out of the earth. The flowers are framed and supported with an armature of river cane. You can make this design with any flowers that have pretty foliage and long stems, such as roses, lilies, gerberas, amaryllises, gladioli, stocks, or sunflowers.

Irises in River Cane

Florals

Five or six river canes, 36"
(91.5 cm) long

Five stems tall, bearded iris

Sheet moss

Tools and materials

Rectangular ceramic container

Marbles or stones for bottom
weight, if needed

Dry floral foam

Knife

Wire cutter

Raffia

Glue gun and glue

1   Weight the bottom of the container with
marbles or stones, if necessary. Cut the foam
so it will fill the container completely from side
to side and sit just below the lip. Secure it into
the container.

2   With the wire cutter, cut at an angle four
pieces of river cane about 2 feet (0.63 m) long.
Glue them into the four corners of the container
at different depths.

3   With the wire cutter, cut at an angle four
pieces of river cane, 10" (25.5 cm) long. With a
touch of hot glue, attach them to the outside of
adjoining upright pieces to make a square that
isn't level.

VARIATION

This design is made with a Paphiopedilum orchid plant on a branch. Faux moss rocks and hanging Spanish moss add to the realism.

4 Tie raffia around the joints to secure the cane and add a rustic look. Cut off the excess raffia and touch the knots with glue.

5 Insert one iris into the center of the foam; insert the other four irises in the corners at the same height, about 1" (2.5 cm) from the armature canes.

6 Place moss around the base of the stems to cover the foam.

7 Look over the design and make any necessary adjustments.

Multiple Flower

TABLE DESIGNS

Designs with more than one kind of flower are versatile and dynamic. They are a chance to play with combinations of colors and textures. Here is a selection of table designs for every season, decorating style, and room. They range from a sweet teapot design to a striking Hawaiian arrangement. Many of the designs will also introduce you to the creative possibilities of unusual containers and accent materials.

Rhapsody in Blue

MIXED HAND-TIED BOUQUET

The technique called hand-tying creates a secure and beautiful bouquet with spiraling stems. A hand-tied bouquet can be made from a single type of flower or with many varieties. This analogous bouquet contains many kinds of long-stemmed blue and purple flowers.

Rhapsody in Blue

Florals

Three stems blue cineraria

Five double stems blue larkspur

Two stems large cosmos

Two stems small cosmos

One bush crassula cut into
ten stems

Two stems blue yarrow

Ten stems variegated hosta foliage

Tools and materials

Anchor tape

Vase

Wire cutter

1 Lay the flowers on the work surface, each type in its own group. Remove the foliage from the lower part of the stems that will be inside the vase.

2 Make a fist with your left hand, thumb outside and facing up. Place a larkspur straight up in your left hand, as if the hand were the vase.

3 Place a second larkspur across the front of the first flower at an angle, with the head left and tail right. (The stem you are adding always goes on top.) Open your thumb and close it over the second stem.

4   Hold your right hand above the left one. Grasp the stems with your right hand, then release the left hand. While holding the flowers in your right hand, make a one-quarter turn clockwise toward your body. Put them back in your left hand.

5   Repeat steps 3 and 4 with the rest of the larkspurs, then repeat with the rest of the stems, choosing at random. End with the hosta leaves.

6   Hold the bouquet in front of you and look at the flowers. Reposition flowers that may have slipped out of place. Move some higher or lower.

7   Tightly wrap the stems with anchor tape above the hand holding the bouquet.

8   Hold the bouquet next to the vase with the flower heads at the height you wish. Cut all the stems even with the bottom of the vase. Put the bouquet in the vase.

VARIATION

This lush bouquet was inspired by wonderful leftovers from summer arrangements. If you keep your extras in four boxes sorted by season, you'll see when it's time to turn them into a new design. This bouquet is made with the hand-tie method; in this case, the bouquet is not secured with tape, but is allowed to spread out for a full look. If you want to reuse the stems, leave them long and bend up the ends before putting them in the vase. Use whatever stems you have on hand, but if you want to duplicate this design, you will need: one bush yellow and brown fever-few, one berry spray cut in half, two stems yellow daisies, one spray blackberry, one spray yellow acacia, one prayer plant, two yellow limonium, one stem green hops, a small bunch of bear grass, and one stem Queen Anne's lace.

All-around Favorite

LOW, ROUND ARRANGEMENT

The most popular flower arrangement of all is a low, rounded mound of flowers. Because this arrangement looks good from any side, it works as a centerpiece and on any table. Choose a neutral container and colors that complement your décor. This version has a traditional Colonial look. The main flowers were purchased as a mixed bush rather than by the stem—a cost-saver.

All-around Favorite

Florals

Bush with twelve single-stemmed mass flowers (roses, hydrangeas, peonies) and foliage

Queen Anne's lace bush with nine single-stemmed flowers and foliage

Sheet moss

Tools and materials

Low, round container

Dry floral foam

Knife

Glue pan and glue

Wire cutter

1 Cut the foam so it will fill the container completely from side to side and sit just below the lip. Secure it into the container.

2 Cut the flowers from the bush so that each stem is the same length and as long as possible. Remove some of the leaves and set aside. Twist and form the rest of the leaves for a natural look.

3 Glue the first stem in the center of the arrangement.

4 Insert four stems toward the edge of the container, evenly spaced around the circle. Drape and bend the flower heads over the lip.

5   Add the rest of the flowers to form an even mound, turning the arrangement as you work.

6   Cut the stems of Queen Anne's lace and insert them at the same height as the main flowers, filling in the spaces between.

7   Cover any gaps between flowers with the reserved foliage. Cover any exposed foam with the moss.

8   Look over the design and make any necessary adjustments.

French Garden

CASUAL ROUND ARRANGEMENT

This is all about pink! A variety of garden flowers fill up a galvanized container and make it lush. The flowers are placed casually and randomly at various heights. Leave each flower long until you try it in the design, then cut the stem. Change the position, too, then glue in place when you're happy. An interesting feature of this design is the soft frame of hosta foliage.

French Garden

2

Florals

Ten stems hosta foliage, each 4" to 5" (10 to 12.7 cm) wide

Three stems wax flower, cut in half

One stem light pink alstroemeria lily

One stem dark pink alstroemeria lily

One stem pink peony

One stem pink kalanchoe

Two stems anemone

Three stems pink freesia

Three stems pink sweet pea

Two stems single white peony with pink tips

Three stems blue cineraria

Tools and materials

Galvanized bucket, about 10" (25.5 cm) across, 6" (15 cm) deep

Floral foam

Knife

Glue pan and glue

Glue gun and glue

Wire cutter

1 Cut the foam so it will fill the container completely from side to side and sit 2" (5 cm) below the lip. Secure it into the container.

2 Place a drop of glue on the underside of one hosta leaf tip and quickly bend the leaf under until it touches the underside of the leaf. Hold in place for a few seconds. Repeat with the rest of the hostas.

3 Insert the hosta stems at an angle into the foam, forming a collar around the container rim.

4 Insert the flowers. Start with the largest peonies, and add the rest in order by size. Space the larger and darker flowers evenly. Keep a loosely rounded shape, but go for a random look and use a variety of heights, cutting the stems apart as you like.

5 Look over the design and make any necessary adjustments.

Watering Can

GARDEN ARRANGEMENT

Garden designs are fresh and casual. This design was inspired by an interesting container, a galvanized tin watering can. It uses a cheerful combination of primary colors—red, blue, and yellow—and the flowers of a summer garden.

Watering Can

Florals

Three stems tall blue lamium

Two stems sunflowers, each with three flowers

Three stems green freesia, each with foliage and two flowers

Three stems red garden roses, each with a blossom and bud

Two stems field grass

One stem novelty foliage

Sheet moss

Tools and materials

Watering can

Container weights

Dry floral foam

Knife

Glue pan and glue

Wire cutter

1 Put the weights into the container. Cut the foam so it will fill the container from side to side and sit 2" (5 cm) above the lip. Secure the foam into the container and cover it with moss.

2 Cut two pieces of the lamium a bit shorter than the third. Insert all three in the center of the foam.

3 Cut long, medium, and short pieces from the sunflower, each with a flower. Insert the longest stem on one side and group the others near it. Curve each stem and bend the heads of the flowers up as if facing the sun.

4 Cut six freesia flowers from the main stem. Cut three pieces of foliage. Insert the freesia and foliage across from the sunflowers at staggered heights. Drape them over the container for a fresh-picked garden look.

5 Cut the roses into three pieces. Insert a large one between the freesia and sunflowers. Add the others at different heights.

6 Cut the grasses and novelty foliage into parts and insert in scattered places.

7 Look over the design and make any necessary adjustments. The main flowers should not touch each other.

Blooming Teapot

DESIGNS IN COLLECTIBLE CHINA

China and ceramics make charming containers for faux floral designs. If you have such a collection, consider highlighting one or more pieces with florals. Small designs in collectible china also make special gifts. Let the container inspire your design. This teapot is sweet and cheerful, and so is the floral design. Wouldn't it make a great Mother's Day present?

Blooming Teapot

Florals

Two stems pink ranunculus, each with three flowers and a bud

One stem white ranunculus, with three flowers and a bud

One stem small, variegated ivy

Tools and materials

Decorative teapot

Dry floral foam

Knife

Glue pan and glue

Two 6" (15 cm) wood picks, wires removed

Green floral tape

Wire cutter

1   Cut the foam so it will fill the container completely from side to side and sit even with the lip. Secure it into the container by the temporary method (page 23).

2   Wrap the blunt ends of two wood picks together with floral tape. Dip the wrapped end of the picks in the glue pan and attach it to the middle underside of the teapot lid. Allow to harden.

3   Insert the pointed ends of the picks into the foam to hold the lid in place, so that the lid is cocked at an angle above the teapot as shown.

4   Cut the flower stems apart. Insert the three largest flower heads in the center of the design just under the lid. Insert the other flowers around the sides.

5   Bend and shape the stems so the flowers dance and flow around the colorful teapot.

3

4

6   Cover the foam and add texture with small pieces of ivy.

7   Look over the design and make any necessary adjustments.

*A teapot that looks like a gourd inspired this autumn design, which includes an 18"
(46 cm) spray of autumn berries cut into six pieces and a small, brightly colored gourd pick with foliage.*

Carnival

A CELEBRATION OF COLORS

Does this remind you of fire-works? Bright, bold colors exploding from a central point create an exciting, energizing arrangement. Dizzy curves of colorful wood string add even more movement.

Carnival

Florals

Five stems purple larkspur

Three stems red ranunculus with one flower and two buds per stem

Three stems yellow freesia with three flowers per stem

Two peony stems

Three stems white/green bouvardia

3 yd. (2.75 m) yellow/gold wood string

2 yd. (1.85 m) burgundy wood string

Tools and materials

Square ceramic container, 6" (15 cm) deep, 6" (15 cm) diameter. 5" (12.7 cm) base

Floral foam

Knife

Glue pan and glue

Wire cutter

1   Cut the foam so it will fill the container from side to side and sit ½" (1.3 cm) above the lip. Secure the foam into the container.

2   Lightly mark crossed lines with your knife into the top of the foam, dividing it into four equal squares. With the knife point, lightly mark the center of each square. In the following steps, the back left square is #1, back right is #2, front right is #3, and front left is #4.

3   Cut a larkspur stem so that it will extend 18" (46 cm) above the foam. Insert it into the center of square #1. Cut another larkspur stem so that it will extend 15" (38 cm) above the foam. Insert it directly in front of the first one, almost in the same place.

4   Cut a larkspur stem so that it will extend 10" (25.5 cm) above the foam. Insert it into the center of square #2. Cut a larkspur stem so that it will extend 12" (30.5 cm) above the foam. Insert it into the center of square #4.

5   Cut the buds from the ranunculus stems. Cut one stem so that it will extend 10" (25.5 cm) above the foam. Cut the second stem so that it will extend 7" (18 cm) and the third stem so that it will extend 5" (12.7 cm). Insert them all in square #2. Bend and shape the large blossoms so they come out and face up to the sun in a stair-step pattern on the right side of the design.

6   Add the ranunculus buds in and around the larger flowers at various heights to create space and depth.

7 Cut the floral stems from the freesia. Insert them at varying lengths in square #4, coming freely out to the side and back. Add foliage around the base of the stems.

8 Cut the peonies so that they extend 5" and 2" (12.7 and 5 cm) above the foam. Insert the tall one in the very center of the design. Insert the short one 2" (5 cm) in front, in square #3, low so the petals are resting on the foam. Cut and add peony foliage to cover the foam and mechanics.

9 Cut each bouvardia stem into three or four pieces. Insert them in and around the center and square #2 to add color, texture, and depth.

10 Cut the wood string into unequal pieces 24" to 30" long (61 to 76 cm); four yellow and three burgundy. For each piece, insert one end into the right side of the foam, arch it naturally across the design front, and insert the other end into the left side. Allow the pieces to "dance to their own music"; some will drape down over the container.

11 Look over the design and make any necessary adjustments.

Christmas Basket

DECORATIVE AND USEFUL

This basket is decorated
around the rim, but the center
is left open to hold a gift of
cookies, candies, gourmet
foods, whatever you like. You
can also use the basket to hold
holiday cards or ornaments.

Christmas Basket

Florals

Garland of poinsettia with greens, berries, and pinecones, 6 ft. (1.85 m) long

Five stems holly with berries

Tools and materials

12" (30.5 cm) basket with handle

Three 24-gauge wires, 18" (46 cm) long

Green floral tape

Wire cutter

Glue pan and glue

24 small holiday balls on wire stems

2 yd. (1.85 m) holiday plaid ribbon

Scissors

1   Open up the garland, bending and twisting the foliage and opening the flowers. Move the cones and berries to look natural. Place the garland around the rim of the basket, folding and placing it where you like. Bring the extra inside the basket as shown or run some up the handle. Wrap the wires with floral tape and cut each into four pieces. Use them to secure the garland to the basket.

2   Cut each holly into three branches. Glue them securely to the basket and garland, both inside and out.

3   Twist pairs of balls together with their wires. Cut the wire to 2" (5 cm) long. Glue the balls to the garland and basket.

4   Weave the ribbon through the design.

5   Look over the design and make any necessary adjustments.

1

European Garden

GROUPING OF INDIVIDUAL POTS

A European garden is a
collection of seasonal blooming
and green plants, each in a
separate container, all placed
in a larger container or basket.
This a casual, garden look
for a family room, screened
porch, or country kitchen.
The design can be as small or
large as you wish.

European Garden

Florals

One miniature ivy plant

One miniature gerbera plant

One small African violet plant

One small ranunculus plant

One miniature daisy plant

One lamb's ear plant

One small variegated pothos

One small baby's tears plant

One small ivy stem

2½" (6.5 cm) bird's nest

Tools and materials

Ceramic container, 9" (23 cm) in diameter and 3" (7.5 cm) deep

8" (20.5 cm) square, 1" (2.5 cm) thick, green Styrofoam

Dry floral foam

Knife

Two 3" (7.5 cm) round clay pots

Three 2" (5 cm) round clay pots

One 1" (2.5 cm) round clay pot

Glue pan and glue

Wire cutter

1 Cut the Styrofoam to cover the bottom of the large container. Glue in place. Glue a smaller square of floral foam to the center of the Styrofoam so the top sits even with the lip.

2 Arrange the small pots in the bigger container, putting some at an angle.

3 Insert a plant into each clay pot, pushing the stem through the center drainage hole into the foam on the bottom to secure it.

4 Insert the pothos, baby's tears, and ivy stem between the blooming plants and drape over the edges. Insert the bird's nest; glue in place.

5 Look over the design and make any necessary adjustments.

3

4

Tiers of Daisies

STACKED CONTAINERS

Daisies are cheerful, casual, country-style flowers. In this design, they are mingled with strawberry vine and stacked in three pots. In choosing the pots, remember that a clay pot is measured across the top inside the clay.

Tiers of Daisies

Florals

Two 12" (30.5 cm) hyacinth stakes

6 ft. (1.85 m) strawberry garland with white flowers and red berries

One bush with white daisies

One bush green miniature daisies

Tools and materials

6" (15 cm) clay pot

4" (10 cm) clay pot

1" to 2" (2.5 to 5 cm) clay pot

Floral foam

Knife

Glue pan and glue

Glue gun and glue

Wire cutter

1 Cut foam for each pot so it will fill completely from side to side and sit even with the lip. Secure foam into each pot.

2 Place the largest pot on the work surface. Place the medium pot on top of it. Place the smallest on the top of the tower. Insert a hyacinth stake into the top pot, through the second, into the third. Make sure the stake does not come out of the bottom of the largest clay pot. If it does, pull it up from the top. Repeat with the second stake. Separate the pots and apply glue with the glue gun where the stakes enter the foam. Push the pots back into position. Cut the stakes 3" (7.5 cm) above the top.

3 Cut the garland into three sections: 3 ft., 2 ft, and 1 ft. (91.5, 61, and 30.5 cm). Dip the end of the shortest piece into the glue pan and insert it into the foam of the smallest pot. Wrap loosely around the pot and glue the other end into the foam. Repeat with the other layers.

4 Cut the daisy and miniature daisy into parts, each 4" (10 cm) long. Insert the stems into and around the pots, but leaving much of the pots exposed. Wrap vine tendrils around the flower heads to hide stems.

5 Look over the design and make any necessary adjustments.

Arid
Garden

A CACTUS ARRANGEMENT

This desert landscape design uses botanically correct arid plants. It can complement a southwestern décor or provide a maintenance-free touch of nature in an office setting.

Arid Garden

Florals

Bunch tall green grass

Dark green grass bush

10" (25.5 cm) senecio plant

5" (12.7 cm) echeveria plant

Dracaena plant

Four small tillandsia plants

12 small dried pods (monkey, lotus, or other)

Tools and materials

Terra-cotta container

Dry floral foam

Knife

Glue pan and glue

Wire cutter

Stones, gravel, sand

1 Cut the foam so it will fill the container completely from side to side and sit 2" (5 cm) below the lip. Secure it into the container.

2 Cut the stems of the plants 2" to 3" (5 to 7.5 cm) long.

3 Arrange the arid plants on the foam without gluing them. Place the tall grass on the far right and the grass bush on the far left, then arrange the smaller plants in a way that looks like a desert landscape. When you are satisfied with the placement, glue the stems and insert them into the foam.

4 Insert the stems of the pods in groups or to form a path through the design.

5 Place the stones in the landscape. Add gravel and sand to cover any exposed foam.

6 Look over the design and make any necessary adjustments.

Purples by Candlelight

CENTERPIECE WITH TAPERS

For this lush centerpiece, choose flowers in a range of purples like red violet and deep blue violet. When using candles in a centerpiece, add them at the beginning so you can see how high and wide you want the design to be. Floral supply stores carry, or can easily order, plastic candlestakes, which are candle holders that include a pick so they can be inserted into floral foam.

Purples by Candlelight

Florals

Six stems leatherleaf fern

Four stems violet morning bells

Three stems white ranunculus

Two stems violet lisianthus

Two stems lady's mantle

Two stems caspia

Three stems red/violet cosmos with three blossoms each

Sheet moss

Tools and materials

Shallow plastic container about 5" × 7" (12.7 × 18 cm)

Dry floral foam

Knife

Glue pan and glue

Two plastic candlestakes

Two 18" (46 cm) white taper candles

Wire cutter

1 Cut the foam so it will fill the container completely from side to side and sit 1½"(3.8 cm) above the lip. Secure it into the container.

2 Insert the candlestakes side by side in the center of the foam, about ½" (1.3 cm) apart. Place the candles in the candlestakes to check the height, then remove them.

3 Cut the leatherleaf into pieces: two pieces 10" (25.5 cm) long, two pieces 8" (20.5 cm) long, two pieces 5" (12.7 cm) long, and three pieces 4" (10 cm) long. Insert one of the longest pieces at the bottom of the side of the foam and extend to one side. Repeat on the opposite side.

4 Place the next longest pieces a bit higher on the foam. Place the 5" (12.7 cm) pieces on top of those. Insert the shortest stems at the candle holders and bend to the front and back of the container. Add in the leftover pieces of the leatherleaf to help cover the foam.

5 Cut the flower stems into pieces at a sharp angle, leaving at least one flower on the main stem and leaving the cut pieces as long as possible.

3

4

5

6   Start adding the flowers, turning the design as you work to view it from all sides. The sides do not need to be identical, but each view should have a good balance of flowers and foliage. Start by placing the two longest morning bells on top of the lowest layer of leatherleaf on each side. Place the remaining morning bells stems on top of each layer, as if they were stairs.

7   Bend and shape the ranunculus stems so the flower and buds look up at the sun. Insert them around the design. Repeat with the cosmos.

8   Insert the caspia, lisianthus, and lady's mantle throughout the design where you want a bit of color and texture.

9   Place the candles in the holders. Look over the design and make any necessary adjustments.

7

Floral Candles

DECORATIVE RINGS

Flowers and foliage arranged around the base of a pillar candle turn it into a charming accent piece. These easy designs make great small table centerpieces for a bridal shower or anniversary celebration. Floral candles can also dress up a buffet for a special dinner party.

Floral Candles

Florals

One stem miniature roses with about ten flowers

16 grapevine leaves

Tools and materials

Cardboard

Compass

Glue gun and glue sticks

1 yd. (0.92 m) ribbon

Scissors

One 24-gauge wire

Round pillar candle, 3" (7.5 cm) diameter

Wire cutter

Glue pan and glue

1   Cut a cardboard circle with a 6" (15 cm) diameter. Draw a 3¼" (8.2 cm) circle in the center; cut out. Remove the plastic spines from the backs of the grapevine leaves and throw them away. Arrange the leaves on the outer ring so they overlap each other slightly, extend beyond the outer edge of the circle, and cover the cardboard completely. Glue in place.

2   Make a bow with the ribbon (page 28). Glue the bow on the grapevine base.

3   Slip the ring over the candle, allowing the leaf edges to come up around the base of the candle.

4   Cut the rose stem into two pieces. Dip the end of one stem in glue and insert it between the back of the bow and the leaf ring (not onto the candle itself). Curve the stem around the candle to the right. Repeat with the other piece, bending it to the left.

5   Look over the design and make any necessary adjustments.

3

4

V A R I A T I O N

Besides a candle and cardboard ring, you will need seven daisies, daisy foliage, and seven corsage pins with pearl heads. You will also need a "work candle." Follow steps 1 and 3, opposite, using about two dozen leaves. Light the work candle. Cut the daisy flowers from the stems, cutting as close as you can to the flower. Hold the sharp end of a pin in the candle flame for five seconds, then immediately push it through the center of a daisy and into the candle near the lower edge. Repeat with the other daisies, forming a circle around the candle.

Christmas Joy

DESIGN ON A CANDLESTICK

An O'dapter, available at florist shops and craft stores, converts a candlestick into an elegant floral holder. This is a dressy Christmas centerpiece, with silver ribbons, velvet poinsettias, and shiny berries.

Christmas Joy

Florals

White hydrangea bush with five flower heads and about twelve leaves

Three stems velvet poinsettias with two large flowers and one small flower each

Two short-needled evergreen branches

Three stems red berries

Tools and materials

Floral foam

Knife

O'dapter

Glue pan and glue

Silver candlestick

Votive candle

Glass votive candle holder

White distilled vinegar

Anchor pin

Scissors

Wire cutter

7 yd. (6.4 m) silver ribbon

Four 18" (46 cm), 24-gauge wires cut in half

1 Cut the foam to fit the O'dapter and glue in place. Place the O'dapter into the candlestick. Put the votive candle in the votive candle holder.

2 Clean the bottom of the glass votive holder with vinegar and dry thoroughly. Attach the anchor pin to the bottom of the holder with hot glue. Dip the anchor pin prongs into the glue pan and then into the top of the foam.

3 Cut single hydrangea leaves. Glue them into the foam, covering the base of the O'dapter.

4 Cut each evergreen branch into six pieces. Insert one on the right side where the foam and holder meet. Repeat on the on the left, front, and back. Insert a piece on the top of the foam next to the glass votive holder, and repeat in the other three sides. Add remaining stems equally all around the foam.

5 Cut each poinsettia into three pieces, each with a flower. Insert four largest pieces next to the four evergreens around the bottom. Keep the stems long and turn the flower heads up toward the sun. Insert rest of the poinsettias near the other branches at the top and throughout the design.

6 Cut the stems of the hydrangea flowers 6" (15 cm) long. Open up and loosen the flowers. Insert them deep in the design, almost touching the foam, on the four sides. Use the last flowers to cover foam where needed. Add hydrangea foliage where you have spaces.

7 Cut the berry stems in three parts each. Insert them all around the design, coming up and down, in and out, bursting with joy and color for the season.

8 Cut the ribbon into 1-yd. (0.92 m) lengths. Form loops in the ends; secure with the 9" (23 cm) wires. Tuck each piece into the design and let it float down.

9 Look over the design and make any necessary adjustments.

Frosted Elegance

SPARKLING ACCENTS

This design captures the perfect winter moment when the sun glitters on icy branches and the evergreens are tipped with new snow. The arrangement includes glittery white roses and branches made of frosted and opalescent beads. This is a sophisticated arrangement to display on an entry table or side table.

Frosted Elegance

Florals

Two full white roses with glittered edges

One branch frosted short-needled evergreen

One branch frosted long-needled evergreen

Six assorted picks miniature evergreens

Beaded stem with three branches

Tools and materials

Tall, thin, decorated vase

Container weights

Dry floral foam

Knife

Glue pan and glue

Wire cutter

1 Put the weights into the container. Cut the foam so it will fill the container completely from side to side and sit just below the lip. Secure it into the container.

2 Cut the rose stems 6" (15 cm) long and 3" (7.5 cm) long. Insert the shorter stem in the front of the design so that the petals touch the foam. Insert the other stem 2" (5 cm) behind and just above. Turn the heads to face up to the sun.

3 Cut each evergreen branch into three pieces.

4 Insert the main stem of the short-needled evergreen at the back left. Arch it from back to front. Add the smaller pieces around its base.

5 Insert the main stem of the long-needled evergreen in the front right corner. Curve it over the front of the vase, then up into the design. Add the remaining pieces around the base to cover the foam.

6 Add the evergreen picks where you like.

7 Insert the beaded stem at the back and right of the design.

8 Look over the design and make any necessary adjustments.

Updated Classic

LOOSENING UP TRADITION

This is a contemporary take on a true classic of floral arranging: the big table piece. The arrangement has been loosened up by mixing in the casual blue flowers and by allowing stems to show. The color scheme is the traditional red, white, and blue, but interpreted in more subtle shades: burgundy, cream, and pastel blue. The wreath on page 187 is a companion piece.

Updated Classic

Florals

Three stems tuberose

Two branches magnolia spray, one white, one white with pink tips

Two stems white hydrangea with pink tips

Two stems cream lilies with three flowers and two buds on each stem

Three white roses with peach tips

Burgundy peony bush with three flowers and one bud

Two stems blue cineraria

Tools and materials

Container

Container weights

Floral foam

Knife

Anchor tape

Three 18" (46 cm), 20-gauge wires

Wire cutter

1   Put the weights into the container. Cut the foam so it will fill the container completely from side to side and sit 2" (5 cm) above the lip. Secure it into the container using anchor tape.

2   Cut the wires into three pieces and set aside.

3   Insert a tuberose stem in the back center of the foam. Cut 3" (7.5 cm) from the second stem and insert at the front left. Cut 4" (10 cm) from the third stem and place at the lower left with the flower head almost touching the foam.

4   Twist the white magnolia stem. Lay the stem on top of the foam with the top of the branch extending to the left and hanging down to almost touch the work surface. Curve three wires into a U shape. Dip in glue and use to secure the stem into the foam. Repeat with the other stem, slightly higher.

5

7

5 Cut the hydrangea stems to 4" (10 cm) long. Insert at the front and center of the foam.

6 Insert one lily stem at the back right between the tuberose and magnolia. Insert the second in front and angle it to the front.

7 Insert the three roses high, medium, and low, spaced evenly like stair steps. Turn them to face the sun.

8 Insert one large peony close to but not touching the magnolia at the right. Insert the second on the lower left between the magnolia stem and the second rose. Place a peony bud higher in the design.

9 Cut the cineraria stems in thirds and add throughout for accent and movement.

10 Look over the design and make any necessary adjustments.

Warm Textures

ABUNDANCE IN AUTUMN COLORS

The wonderful textures of the flowers come forward in this arrangement because the florals are all warm colors in an analogous color scheme. This is a lush, impressive arrangement that is designed in a formal linear shape known to floral designs as a Hogarth curve. Its lure keeps your eyes moving from one area to another.

Warm Textures

Florals

Three stems yellow gladiolus

Two stems large yellow spider chrysanthemums

Two stems large sunflower

Two branches crabapple

Four stems orange spray roses with one flower and two buds each

One branch rose hips

Three stems black-eyed Susan, four flowers each

Two stems yellow and cream alstroemeria lily with four flowers and three buds each

Three stems field grass

One small bush variegated pothos

Tools and materials

Vase

Container weights

Newspaper

Dry floral foam

Glue pan and glue

1 Put the weights into the container. Add crumpled newspapers to take up space. Cut the foam so it will fill the top of the container completely from side to side and sit 2"(5 cm) above the lip. Secure the foam into the container.

2 Cut ½" (1.3 cm) from the bottom of a gladiolus stem and insert at the center back of the foam. Cut 2" (5 cm) from the bottom of the second gladiolus stem and insert it in front of and to the right of the first, angled to the front. Cut 3" (7.5 cm) from the third gladiolus stem and insert it to the left and angled to the front.

3 Cut the stem of one chrysanthemum 6" (15 cm) long. Insert with the flower facing up at the base of the gladiolus. Cut the stem of the second chrysanthemum 10" (25.5 cm) long. Bend its face to the sky, curve the stem, and insert near the first, curving it over the lip of the vase. Cut a sunflower stem 6" (15 cm) long and insert it on the far left of the design so the bottom of the flower lays flat on the foam. Cut the second sunflower stem 10" (25.5 cm) long and insert it above the other one.

4 Cut 1" (2.5 cm) from one the end of one crabapple branch and 2" (5 cm) from the other. Insert in the foam near the gladiolus stems and bend in a crescent shape.

5 Cut 2" (5 cm) from the rose sprays. Insert the four sprays into the front right side. Bend and shape the stems down over the vase; separate the large roses so each has space to shine. Insert the rose hips among the roses.

6 Bend and shape the black-eyed Susan stems. Insert two on the left, the third on the right.

7 Cut 3" (7.5 cm) from the stem of one alstroemeria and insert it between the gladiolus and rose. Cut 6" (15 cm) from the second lily and insert it in front of the other one at an angle.

8 Cut 3" and 6" (7.5 and 15 cm) from the field grass stems. Insert near the lilies, keeping the stems separate.

9 Cut and insert the pothos around the design to cover the foam and mechanics.

10 Look over the design and make any necessary adjustments.

Verticals in Yellow

STRONG VERTICAL DESIGN

Like Warm Textures on page 123, this contemporary design uses all yellow florals—but differently! What's fascinating here is the strongly vertical line—starting with the heavy lilies that point upward just above the vase, then traveling with the orchids as they wind their way up the tall bamboo.

Verticals in Yellow

Florals

Six pencil stems lucky bamboo

One branch faux curly willow with several small stems

One stem Oncidium orchid with three branches

One stem lily with two flowers and two buds

One bromeliad plant with foliage and grasses

Sheet moss

Tools and materials

Narrow ceramic vase

Container weights

Dry floral foam

Knife

Glue pan and glue

Wire cutter

1   Put the weights into the container. Cut the foam so it will fill the container completely from side to side and sit just above the lip. Secure it into the container.

2   Insert the six bamboo stems in the center of the foam close together.

3   Cut two small stems from the main willow branch. Insert the main branch to the left of the lucky bamboo and wrap it up around the bamboo. Insert the smaller willow stems at the same spot, then bring them down to hug the lower part of the vase.

4   Glue the orchid into the foam on the right, next to the bamboo. Wrap the orchid stems up and around the bamboo randomly.

5 Cut the lily flowers and buds from the stems, leaving 3" (7.5 cm) of stem attached to each. Insert the flowers into the foam so their bases touch the foam and the tips point straight up.

6 Separate the bromeliad and grass stem into bunches. Insert them on the opposite side from the largest lily flower.

7 Add moss to cover any exposed foam. Touch the two willow stems curling around the vase with a dab of glue and add small pieces of moss to conceal the glue.

8 Look over the design and make any necessary adjustments.

Hawaii!

DRAMATIC TROPICAL FLORALS

Each of these colorful tropical flowers has the space to show off. The lines and angles of this design are more exacting than those of many kinds of arrangements. Look for a container that complements the flowers. The exotic-looking grass spheres are a product made by softening long, fine reeds and forming them into a ball.

Hawaii!

Florals

One stem hanging heliconia

Two stems bird-of-paradise

Two stems red anthurium

Two stems Dendrobium orchids

Two stems yellow pincushion protea

One stem yellow kangaroo paw with four branches

Three 2" (5 cm) mustard colored grass spheres

Two stems tropical foliage

Sheet moss

Tools and materials

Ceramic vase

Container weights

Dry floral foam

Knife

Glue pan and glue

Wire cutter

1   Put the weights into the container. Cut the foam so it will fill the container completely from side to side and sit 1" (2.5 cm) below the lip of the container. Secure it into the container.

2   Insert the heliconia at the back in the center. Arch the flower forward and down.

3   Remove the leaves from the stems of the birds-of-paradise and set aside. Insert the longer floral stem in the back of the foam and the second one, 2" (5 cm) shorter, at the front. Point the tips of the flowers toward the heliconia.

4   Insert the anthuriums in the front left corner. Bend the stems to create a look of movement with the flowers pointing to the design center.

5   Cut the two orchids each into three pieces. Insert at the front left in a grouping, and let the flowers hang down naturally.

6   Cut the protea stems 3" (7.5 cm) long. Remove the leaves and set aside. Place the protea, one in

front of the other, in front of the heliconia stem, with the front one 1" (2.5 cm) higher.

7   Insert the kangaroo paw in the back right corner. Arch the stem back, then forward.

8   Cut the reserved protea foliage into three pieces and use it to cover the foam. Glue the grass spheres in a triangle at the right front corner. Insert the birds-of-paradise leaves behind the heliconia so that they touch at the base but not at the top.

9   Add a tropical leaf in the back right corner. Bring it over the top of the protea and grass spheres, like an umbrella. Mirror it with the other tropical foliage, set further back and at the same angle.

10   Glue pieces of sheet moss over any exposed areas of foam. Look over the design and make any necessary adjustments.

Topiaries
AND BRANCHES

Arrangements with dried or faux branches bring nature inside. The look can be woodsy, but as two of these designs show, it can also be contemporary. Branches can also be used to form the stem of a topiary (a compact sphere of floral material atop a slender stem in a small container). These designs include traditional ivy and rosebud topiaries, plus unusual garden and modern topiaries. In decorating, topiaries are traditionally shown in pairs, though some work fine alone.

Ivy Topiary

THE STEM AND BALL

This natural-looking ivy topiary is made of both dried and permanent botanicals. The stem is three small natural branches of birch or willow. Choose dry branches with some bends and twists to give the piece personality.

Ivy Topiary

Florals

Three slender natural branches, each 1 ft. (30.5 cm) long

Ivy bush with medium-sized leaves

Moss

Tools and materials

Rustic container

Styrofoam or dry floral foam

Knife

Glue pan and glue

Utility snips

One 18" (46 cm), 24-gauge wire

Brown floral tape

Wire cutter

1 Cut the foam so it will fill the container completely from side to side and sit just below the lip. Secure it into the container.

2 Insert the branches into the center of the foam.

3 Cut two stems from the ivy bush and set aside. Cut the remaining bush 2" (5 cm) below the point where all the stems join together. Wrap the wire with the floral tape (page 26). Place the tops of the branches around the cut end of the bush; wrap with wire to secure.

4 Glue moss over the wired area of the branches using a honey stick (page 25) to hide the mechanics.

5 Shape the ivy stems into a rounded ball. Cut off a few small ivy sprigs here and there.

6 Cut each of the reserved stems into two pieces. Insert one piece into each side of the foam at the base of the branches. Glue small ivy sprigs here and there on the branches.

7 Glue moss around the base to cover the foam and mechanics.

8 Look over the design and make any necessary adjustments.

Miniature Rose Topiary

FLORAL TOPIARIES

Faux florals can be used to create wonderful floral topiaries. For stability, these branches are anchored in plaster of Paris. This design is small and sweet— perfect for a dresser or night table. You can make a pair (or triplet) for a larger table.

Miniature Rose Topiary

Florals

Five 9" (23 cm) dried branches
(birch, willow, dogwood)

One bush miniature roses with
24 flowers and foliage

Tools and materials

Small clay pot

Plaster of Paris

Flocking adhesive and
green flocking

Utility snips

One 18" (46 cm), 24-gauge wire
cut in half

Wire cutter

Green floral tape

2" (5 cm) moss-covered foam
sphere

Glue pan and glue

Awl

1   Plug the hole in the bottom of the pot.
Mix plaster of Paris and pour into the pot to 1/2"
(1.3 cm) below the rim.

2   Insert the branches in the center of the plaster.
Hold them straight up until the plaster is firm.
Allow plaster to harden. Apply flocking adhesive
and flocking to top and sides of pot, following the
manufacturer's directions.

3   Wrap a wire with the floral tape (page 26).
Place the wrapped wire 1" (2.5 cm) from the top
of the branches and gently pull the tops together.
Twist the wire together to secure the bundle.
Bend the lose ends into the branches.

4   Place the sphere on top of the branches and
push it about 1" (2.5 cm) deep. Secure with glue.

4

6

5 Cut the roses from the bush, leaving each with a stem ½" (1.3 cm) long.

6 Insert the roses into the sphere by making a hole with the awl, dipping a stem in the glue, and gently inserting it into the hole. Insert them evenly all around the ball.

7 Insert rose foliage to cover gaps between the roses.

8 Look over the design and make any necessary adjustments.

Cascade
of Geraniums

GARDEN-STYLE TOPIARY

In this casual garden design, brilliant red geraniums cascade from the top of a column of birch branches. Once you've created the stem, you can easily switch the flowers for seasonal variations. Try mums in the fall or pansies in the spring.

Cascade of Geraniums

Florals

15 to 20 natural dried branches, willow or birch, about 20" (51 cm) long

Sheet moss

Two hanging geranium plants, 12 stems each

Tools and materials

Tall clay pot with 6" (15 cm) top, and 4" (10 cm) base

Container weights

Dry floral foam

Knife

Utility snips

Glue pan and glue

One 18" (46 cm), 24-gauge wire

Brown floral tape

Wire cutter

2

1 Put the weights into the container. Cut the foam so it will fill the container completely from side to side and sit just above the lip. Secure it into the container.

2 Cut the ends of the branches at an angle. Place the first branch in the center of the foam. Working out from the center, place the others around it in a circle. Depending on the branches you are using, the finished circle will be 2" to 4" (5 to 10 cm) wide. Cut the branches even at the top.

3 Wrap the wire with the floral tape (page 26). Wrap the wire around the branches 1" (2.5 cm) from the top and gently pull the branch tops together while still allowing them to stand straight

up and down. Twist the wire together to secure the bundle. Bend any loose ends into the branches. (Do not cut them, as you'll create a sharp point that could hurt someone.)

4 Cover the foam with moss. Glue some moss to the outside of the pot for a natural look.

5 Cut apart one geranium plant, keeping the stems as long as possible—2" to 4" (5 to 10 cm) depending on the bush. Insert two of the stems into the foam and hang them over the pot.

6 Bend the rest of the cut branches about 3" (7.5 cm) from the bottom. Place these branches into the top of the branch column and hang them down.

7 Insert the second geranium plant into the top of the branches. Bend and drape the stems to create bulk and dimension.

8 Look over the design and make any necessary adjustments.

Contemporary Topiaries

A NEW INTERPRETATION

This is a new take on the topiary. In this delicate design, the stem is a reed bundle and the ball is a single round flower. The vases are filled with sand to add weight, anchor the reeds, and add a decorative element. Use fine-grained craft sand, either natural or colored. You can change the flowers with the seasons.

Contemporary Topiaries

Florals

One natural reed bundle, about 30 stems

Four stems cream parchment hydrangea without the leaves

Tools and materials

Two thin, clear glass vases

Funnel

Cream-colored sand

Anchor tape

5 yd. (4.6 m) each of two coordinating ribbons

24-gauge wire

1 Divide the reed bundle into two smaller bundles. Place each in a vase.

2 Holding the reeds, pour the sand through the funnel into the vases until the reeds are held securely upright.

3 Open up and spread out the hydrangeas. Place two hydrangeas in the center of each reed bundle. Secure the bundle with anchor tape, ½" (1.3 cm) from the top.

4 Cut each piece of ribbon in half. Holding two different ribbons together, make a bow as on page 28, leaving long tails. Repeat with the remaining two ribbons. Wire the bows to the top of the reeds over the tape. Let the tails pool at the bottom of the vase.

1

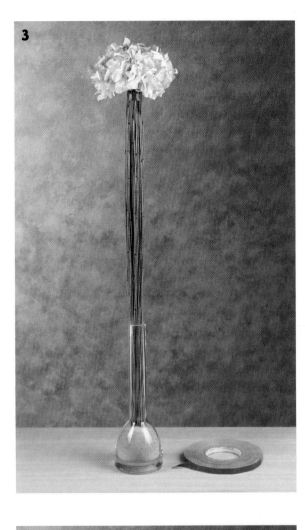

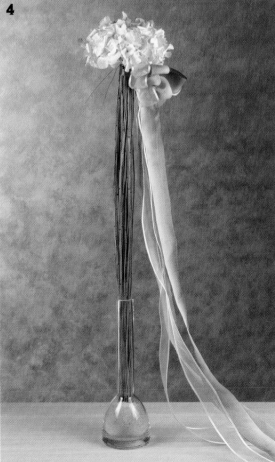

151

Cardinals in the Branches

PINECONES AND MUSHROOM BIRDS

Tiny mushroom birds add color and whimsy to a floral design. This woodland scene is perfect for winter decorating in a cabin or den. You can make a similar design on a much larger scale to surround a window; secure thicker branches into containers on both sides of the window, and attach cross branches with thick wire.

Cardinals in the Branches

Florals

Garland of mixed evergreens with pinecones and red berries, 3 ft. (1 m) long

Six 3-ft. (1-m) branches, birch or a mixture

Large western pinecone

Two evergreen branches with three stems each

Sheet moss

Purchased bird's nest

Flock of mushroom cardinals (seven to twelve)

Tools and materials

Rectangular container

Dry floral foam

Knife

Glue pan and glue

Utility snips

Awl

One 9" (23 cm) wood pick, wire removed

Brown floral tape

Four 18" (46 cm), 26-gauge wires

Wire cutter

1   Cut the foam so it will fill the container completely from side to side and sit just below the lip. Secure it into the container.

2   Bend and shape the evergreen garland around the base of the container. Twist the branches through and around each other. Bend some branches below the lip of the container and across the top of the foam.

3   Cut the tree branches in half, don't trim the offshoots. Insert three of the bottom parts in the foam on the far right side. Repeat on the left.

4 With the awl, make a hole in the end of the large cone. Glue the blunt end of the wood pick into the hole. Insert the cone on the left side of the design.

5 Wrap the wire with the floral tape (page 26). Cut each into fourths. You will use these wires to connect the horizontal canopy.

6 On the work surface, lay the tops of the branches together, alternating the direction. Connect them together with wires, forming a sort of canopy of branches. Instead of cutting the ends of the wire, curl them around your finger or a pencil so they look like trailing vines.

7 Pick up the canopy and gently place it in position as shown. Attach the canopy to the side branches with twists of wire.

8 Insert the two evergreen branches into the foam on the opposite side from the big cone. Bend and twist the stems.

9 Place moss on the foam and in and around the evergreens. Instead of pressing down, let it fluff realistically.

10 Glue the nest to a sturdy stem. Glue the cardinals on the branches, facing them in different directions.

11 Look over the design and make any necessary adjustments.

Blooming Branches

LARGE FLOOR DESIGN

Permanent botanical branches
are flexible, so they're easy
to shape. You will find many
types of branching stems, with
and without seasonal flowers.
Flocked branches, with a light-
green latex coating, can add
texture. Including both tall and
short branches gives depth and
dimension to the design. Choose
a container that's heavy—both
physically and visually.

Blooming Branches

Florals

Two branches faux willow, 5 ft. (1.58 m) long

Five branches faux willow, 4 ft. (1.23 m) long

10 to 15 dried birch branches, 3 to 6 ft. (0.92 to 1.85 m) long

Two flocked branches with multiple stems

Tools and materials

Large heavy floor vase

Container weights

Chicken wire

Garden gloves

1 Put weights into the container. Wrap the chicken wire around your hand several times. Push it down into the vase, leaving some even with the top.

2 Twist, bend, and shape the willows. Insert them through the chicken wire so they reach up and out to the sides.

3 Add the birch branches in and between the willows, spreading them out at the top in a wide angle. Place enough stems through the chicken wire to hold them all firmly.

4 Insert flocked stems around the outer edge of the design.

5 Look over the design and make any necessary adjustments.

Hidden in the Branches

A MYSTERIOUS FLOOR DESIGN

Put this contemporary design in a hall or entrance and people will stop to peer into it! The coiled copper wire (called bullion) catches the light and draws your attention. The design has an air of mystery—what's hiding inside those branches? It's great for high-traffic areas because nothing sticks out to trip passersby.

Hidden in the Branches

Florals

Five 3-ft. (0.92 m) stems
red gladiolus

Three stems open red roses

Three stems red rosebuds

Six small red anthurium

Sheet moss

12 natural branches such as birch,
each 48" (122 cm) long

Tools and materials

Tall container; the one shown is
24" (61 cm) tall, 12" (30.5 cm)
across at the top

Container weights

Newspaper

Dry floral foam

Knife

Glue pan and glue

Wire cutter

Utility snips

Four strands copper bullion, each
12" (30.5 cm) long

1 Put the weights into the container. Add crumpled newspapers. Cut the foam so it will fill the container completely from side to side and sit just below the lip. Secure it into the container.

2 Insert a gladiolus stem in the center of the foam. Insert the other four stems 1" (2.5 cm) from each corner. Face all the flowers to the outside.

3 Cut the stems of the open roses long, medium, and short. Insert them on three different sides with the flowers facing out. Cut and insert the rosebuds the same way. Turn the design as you place the flowers; the pattern is up to you, as long as the flowers are all vertical at different heights.

4 Cut the anthurium stems different lengths, ranging from 2" (5 cm) stems to the whole stem. Place as you did the roses.

5 Cover the foam by working small pieces of moss between the stems.

6 Cut the branches at an angle, most of them around 4 ft. (1.23 m) and some shorter. Insert the taller branches around the edge of the container. Work the moss around the branches as you go. Add the shorter branches to fill in the spaces, but leave small openings.

7 Attach a piece of copper bullion to the bottom of a branch. Stretching the coil gently, wrap the outside of the branches, moving up and down and crisscrossing the design. Do not wrap too tightly; the branches should stay vertical, and the center of the stems should not curve in. Tie the end of the bullion to another branch. Repeat with the other pieces of bullion, crossing over the other wires in an irregular pattern.

8 Look over the design and make any necessary adjustments.

Wreaths
AND WALL DESIGNS

Wreaths don't have to be round. Square and oval wreaths are popular, too. There are also many kinds of swags. A swag can be a wild tangle of grapevines or a lush, lavish length of evergreens and gilded fruits and florals. Some of the designs in this group begin with a purchased base, and others are created from branches or floral stems. Whatever you make, hang the piece while you're working on it so you see the natural fall of the materials.

Wreath with Bird's Nest

WREATH BASICS

If you try to make this wreath while it's lying on the work surface, you'll probably place the nest in such a position that the eggs will fall out when you hang the finished wreath! This project introduces you to the techniques of working with grapevine wreaths and honeysuckle vines.

Wreath with Bird's Nest

Florals

12" (30.5 cm) round grapevine wreath

4 ft. (1.23 m) honeysuckle vine

2 stems flocked curly willow with leaves, each 4 ft. (1.23 m) long

Purchased bird's nest

Stem peony with two large blossoms, three buds, and foliage

Stem variegated ivy with three vines

Four small eggs

Tools and materials

Ten 18" (46 cm), 26-gauge wires

Brown floral tape

Wire cutter

Glue pan and glue

1 Divide the grapevine wreath into two wreath bases, following the instructions on page 26. Set one aside for another project.

2 Wrap the honeysuckle vine around the wreath base, weaving the vines together and mixing the colors and textures of the grapevine and honeysuckle. Leave spaces between the vines to give the wreath visual texture and depth. Secure the vines together with the taped wire as in step 4, page 27. Make sure the structure is secure all the way around.

3 Attach a hanger to the wreath, following the instructions on page 27.

4 Gently bend and shape flocked curly willow. Shape the leaves. Wrap the willow branches

5

7

around the grapevine and honeysuckle, adding a
new texture. Secure with taped wire. Coil the
taped wire ends to resemble tendrils.

5 Place the nest in the lower right-hand corner.
Glue it in place with hot glue.

6 Cut the peony stem into four pieces. Glue the
two large flowers into the base of the wreath,
one in front below the nest, the second to the
back left of the nest.

7 Glue a peony bud coming out from the lower
left. Glue the second out near the edge of the
vine and the third slightly higher on the edge.

8 Cut the ivy stem into three parts and glue them
into the base of the nest. Glue the eggs in the nest.

9 Glue the peony foliage into and around the
left side of the nest and around the peony buds
to hide the mechanics.

10 Look over the design and make any necessary
adjustments

Hanging Square

EVERGREEN WREATH WITH EXTRAS

Hanging a wreath with heavy tapestry roping creates a luxurious look. You can make this handsome square wreath using ornaments and cones for the holidays, or other materials for use year-round. Like many wreaths, this also can be used as a table design. The neeto vine is a natural material sold in craft and floral stores.

Hanging Square

Florals

18" (46 cm) square grapevine wreath

Garland of mixed evergreens with pinecones and red berries, 6 ft. (2.75 m) long

Four evergreen picks, three branches each

1 yd. (0.92 m) neeto vine in multiple bunches, 3" (7.5 cm) wide

Tools and materials

3 yd. (2.75 m) heavy red tapestry rope

Nine holiday ornaments

Nine pinecones

Glue pan and glue

1   Hang the grapevine wreath at your work space. Place the garland on top of the vine wreath all around. In each corner, weave a small evergreen stem from the garland through a strong grapevine branch, and twist it together with another evergreen stem to secure.

2   Insert evergreen picks in and around the grapevine. Instead of gluing the picks in place,

secure them by wrapping with stems of evergreen, as in step one.

3 Fold the tapestry rope in half. Tie the doubled rope in a knot about 6" (15 cm) from the fold, forming a loop for hanging. Secure a rope tail to each upper corner of the wreath, about 18" (46 cm) below the knot, by winding an evergreen stem tightly around it. Let the free rope ends hang down.

4 Separate out pieces of neeto vine. Spread the pieces in and around the evergreen garland.

5 Glue on the pinecones and holiday ornaments, if desired, either in a pattern or randomly.

6 Look over the design and make any necessary adjustments.

Formal Wreath

FOR TRADITIONAL DÉCORS

This wreath belongs in a living room or dining room with a traditional décor. Its formality comes from the deep colors and the flower choices—hydrangeas always look top-drawer. The wreath can be hung with the exposed grapevine on the top, bottom, or side. If the wreath will be seen from the sides and bottom as well as the front, make sure you put flowers in all these areas.

Formal Wreath

Florals

20" (51 cm) grapevine wreath

Two stems burgundy cockscomb

Two stems burgundy berries with six branches per stem

Three stems green hydrangea

One large burgundy rose

Two sprays burgundy wild mini lily

Three stems burgundy freesia with three flowers per stem

One hanging green amaranthus with three stems

Tools and materials

Newspaper

Glossy wood-tone spray

Four 18" (46 cm), 26-gauge wires

Brown floral tape

Glue gun and sticks

Wire cutter

1 Lay the wreath on newspaper in a well-ventilated area. Clean and shine the wreath front and back with the glossy wood-tone spray. This gives the wreath a slightly more formal varnished look. Allow to dry for a few minutes. Wrap the wires with floral tape; cut them into four pieces.

2 Hang the wreath in your work area. Wrap the cockscomb stems around your hand, and stretch them into loose coils. Secure them to the wreath front, with one blossom on the left and one on the right. Wire the stems to the wreath where they touch. Tuck the stem ends into the wreath at the bottom center; glue in place.

3 Place one stem of berries on the right side of the wreath. Shape it to curve like the wreath, and weave the stem through the cockscomb stem coils and into the grapevine; glue in place. Set aside the other berry stem.

4 Cut two of the hydrangea stems 5" (12.7 cm) long; remove the foliage. Insert the stems, pointing toward each other, in the center bottom of the wreath, forming one large blossom; glue in place. Set aside the other hydrangea.

5 Cut the rose stem 5" (12.7 cm) long. Glue it to the left of the hydrangea, facing the rose left and out.

6 Place one wild lily spray on the upper left. Shape it to curve like the wreath, and weave the stem through the cockscomb stem coils and into the grapevine. Glue it in place. Place the second spray below the first and glue in place.

7 Cut each freesia into three pieces. Glue them randomly in and around the other stems. Cut the remaining hydrangea into florets. Glue them around the wreath where some light color and texture is needed. Use the hydrangea foliage previously set aside to cover any mechanics that are showing.

8 Cut the amaranthus and remaining berry stem into several parts. Tuck them in where you want to add color and texture; glue in place.

9 Look over the design and make any necessary adjustments.

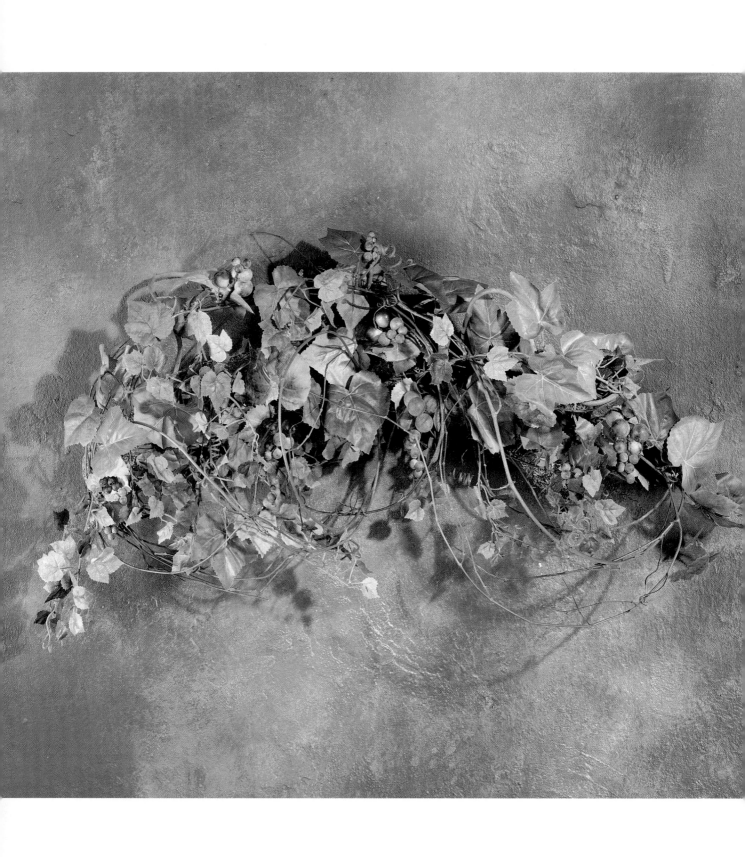

Vineyard Swag

NATURAL AND FAUX GRAPEVINES

This easy project is a good introduction to working with natural grapevine. It starts with a purchased base and includes faux grapevines from a bush. The vines are secured with lots of wrapped wire, which builds a secure swag that will be beautiful for a long time.

Vineyard Swag

Florals

3 ft. (0.92 m) natural coiled, dried grapevine

Faux grapevine garland with six branches and small grape clusters

Tools and materials

Six 18" (46 cm), 24-gauge wires

Green floral tape

36" (0.92 m) Styrofoam swag form covered with moss

Glue gun and glue sticks

1   Wrap each of the wires with floral tape (page 26). Cut each wire into four pieces. Bend half of the pieces into a U-shape.

2   Separate the natural coiled grapevine into individual vines. Lay one piece at a time on top of the swag form and work it around, letting it twist and turn naturally. Secure wherever the grapevine touches the foam with a U-shaped wire dipped in glue.

3   Cut the grapevine garland into three pieces. Attach one section to the swag form, using U-shaped wired dipped in glue.

4   Drape and work the remaining grapevine pieces around the natural grapevine, front to back, in and out for depth. Secure them to the grapevine with the straight wires, leaving the wire ends long.

5   Curl and twist the wire ends to resemble real vine tendrils.

6   Hang the swag. Look over the design and make any necessary adjustments.

Magnolia Swag

A FEMININE SWAG

This lovely swag is built on a base of willow branches. It's easy to make and requires little material. The magnolias make it a dressy design that would be wonderful in a bedroom. Or lay it down the middle of a table and add a couple of candles.

Magnolia Swag

Florals

Ten small natural branches of various lengths

Two magnolia stems, each with two large, medium, and small flowers

Garland grape ivy with grape clusters and multiple offshoots, 6 ft. (1.85 m) long

Tools and materials

Utility snips

Six 18" (46 cm), 24-gauge wires

Brown floral tape

One 18" (46 cm), 21-gauge wire

Wire cutter

1 Lay the branches on the work surface, with some tips to the right, some to the left. Use the with the same number of branches on each side so the swag will be balanced.

2 Wrap the 24-gauge wire with tape (page 26) and cut each into four pieces. Secure the branches together with twists of the taped wire.

3 Hang the swag in your work area. Continue to secure the branches with wires until the swag feels secure when you shake it a bit.

4 Turn the swag over and make a hanger with the 21-gauge wire (page 27).

5 Rehang the swag in your work area. Twist and curl the magnolia stems into a coil; do not cut the stems. Place one with the flowers to the left. Curl the stem into the branches and secure with wrapped wire. Repeat with the other stem, this time with the flowers to the right.

5

6 Cut the ivy garland in half. Weave the ivy through the design and let the ends drape from the ends of the swag. Secure with taped wire, letting some ivy flow free and attaching some tightly to the branches.

7 Look over the design and make any necessary adjustments.

6

Oval Wreath

UPDATED CLASSIC

This wreath was designed to complement the table arrangement on page 119. Envision the urn on the far left of a mahogany sideboard, and this oval wreath on the right side, about ten inches from the table top. Fabulous! When you make one arrangement for a special place, consider making a companion piece from the same florals and style elements.

Oval Wreath

Florals

Four kiwi vines

Two magnolia sprays, one white,
one white with pink tips

Two stems cream lilies

Two stems white hydrangea
with pink tips

Two burgundy peony bunches
with two flowers and foliage
on each

Two stems blue cineraria

Tools and materials

Six 18" (46 cm), 24-gauge wires

Brown floral tape

Wire cutter

Glue pan and glue

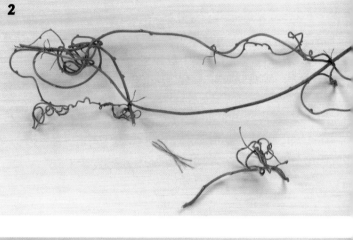

1   Wrap the wires with floral tape (page 26).
Cut each into four pieces.

2   Form an oval wreath base with the kiwi
stems, twisting them together at the outer corners.
The upper and lower arches of the wreath
should be slightly shorter than the magnolia
stems. Secure them together where they touch,
using covered wire.

3   Lay the magnolia stems over the kiwi vines,
one end to the left, the other to the right. Connect
them to the kiwi in several places with taped wires.

5

8

4   Place two hangers on the back of the wreath (page 27), a few inches (centimeters) apart at the top center. Wrap the wires around the kiwi and magnolia stems. Hang the wreath.

5   Twist and curl the lilies. Place one along the bottom of the wreath, flowers to the left. Secure with taped wire in four places. Place the second with the head to the top right and secure.

7   Remove the hydrangea heads and foliage from the stems. Glue one head at the wreath bottom and one at the top. Tuck the leaves in behind the flowers.

8   Cut the heads from the peonies. Glue one to the right of the bottom hydrangea and the other to the left of the top hydrangea. Use the foliage from the peonies to hide any visible mechanics throughout the design.

9   Cut each cineraria stem into four parts. Hang and drape them throughout. Glue in place.

10   Look over the design and make any necessary adjustments.

Gilded Swag

METALLIC ACCENTS

This opulent swag belongs above an armoire or buffet, along a fireplace mantle, or down the center of a dining table. The design brings together golds and coppers and includes elegant silk skeletonized leaves. You can bend and twist the materials into the evergreen instead of using glue. That way, you can reuse the garland and flowers in future arrangements.

Gilded Swag

Florals

Evergreen garland,
6 ft. (1.85 m) long

Holly garland edged with gold,
6 ft. (1.85 m) long

Five gilded rose picks

Six gilded fruit picks

Three branches gold skeletonized leaves

Tools and materials

6 yd. (5.5 m) copper-gilded ribbon

Three 18" (46 cm), 24-gauge wires

Green floral tape

1   Make a looped bow with streamers (page 28), using 3 yd. (2.75 m) of ribbon. Place the bow in the center of the evergreen garland and twist evergreen around it to secure.

2   Lay the holly garland over the evergreen garland, intermingling the foliage. Secure the garlands together in several places with twists of evergreen stems.

3   Place the five gilded rose picks on top of the garland, finding the right spot for each. Leaving the stems on, tuck the pick into the place you've chosen. Bend and shape the flowers to bring them to life. Wrap two pieces of evergreen tightly around the stem of each pick.

4   Place the gilded fruit picks on the garland, and wrap as you did the roses. Twist and pull the evergreens around the additions for a full look.

5   Cut each stem of gold leaves into several parts. Tuck them around the garland, including next to the bow.

4

5

6 Loop and weave the remaining ribbon through the garland, attaching it where you choose with twists of evergreen stems.

7 Look over the design and make any necessary adjustments.

Garden Plaque

BACKING WITH FOLIAGE

This plaster plaque came with a wire cage on the back to hold the foam for the design. You can hang the finished design on a wall or door or place it on a mantle, table, doorway, or shelf.

Garden Plaque

Florals

Sheet moss

One bunch long grass

One branch permanent curly willow with foliage

Four stems blackberry with foliage

Three stems green preserved beech

Tools and materials

Garden plaque with wire cage

Floral foam

Knife

Glue gun and glue

Wire cutter

1   Place sheet moss around the inside of the cage. Cut the foam to fit snugly inside the moss. Gently insert the foam. Glue in place.

2   Turn the plaque to the front. Insert the grass bunch to the right of center.

3   Cut the curly willow in five pieces. Insert two coming from the top right and draping to the right. Insert three on the left draping to the side.

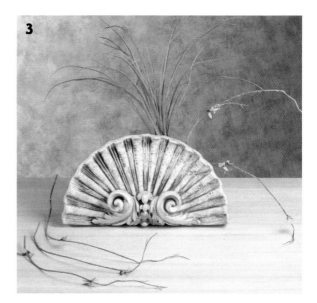

4 Cut each blackberry stem in two. Bend and shape them. Insert four on the left and four on the right.

5 Cut each beech into three pieces. Insert them throughout the design to add texture.

6 Look over the design and make any necessary adjustments.

Autumn Wall Basket

SEASONAL DISPLAY

This is an autumn design with muted oranges, reds, and golds, and seasonal touches of kale and pheasant feathers. The hanging sedum sways in a breeze, adding motion. The basket has been touched with paint to add texture. Hang this large basket over a fireplace or in a nook where people won't bump into it.

Autumn Wall Basket

Florals

Two stems yellow leper lilies, 24" (61 cm) long

One decorative kale

Three stems grape-colored open roses, 18" (46 cm) long

Two orange gerberas, 12" (30.5 cm) long

Two stems yellow ranunculus

Three orange spray roses, six flowers on each stem

Three stems hanging sedum

Three sprays autumn-colored eucalyptus foliage

Tools and materials

Hanging green vine wall basket with handle, 12" (30.5 cm) long, 6" (15 cm) wide, 10" (25.5 cm) deep

Newspaper

Plastic bag or disposable gloves

Whitewash paint

Disposable plastic plate

Floral foam

18" (46 cm) square of green plant foil

Wood picks

Six to eight pheasant feathers

1 Lay the basket on newspaper in a well-ventilated area. Put on the gloves. Spray a puddle of whitewash on a plastic plate. Dip your fingers in the puddle and dab the paint over the basket and handle here and there, leaving touches of white. The paint will dry in seconds.

2 Insert foam into the basket to just below the lip, following the directions on page 24.

3 Hang the basket. Cut 2" (5 cm) from the first lily stem and insert it straight up in the center back of the foam. Cut 4" (10 cm) from the second stem and insert in front, a bit to the right, and at a slight angle. Insert the kale so the face points up and the bottom touches the foam.

4 Cut 2" (5 cm) from one rose stem and insert in front of the lily at a slight angle. Cut 4" (10 cm) from the second stem and insert it in front of the first. Cut 6" (15 cm) from the third stem and insert it the left of the first rose, angled toward the front at a 45-degree angle.

5 Cut 3" (7.5 cm) from one gerbera stem; cut 6" (15 cm) from the other. Insert them on the left side. Bend one below the edge of the basket, the other away from the basket.

6 Cut 2" (5 cm) from one ranunculus stem; cut 4" (10 cm) from the other. Insert them at the lower right. Drape one over the side.

7 Insert one spray rose stem on the left side. Cut the others into smaller pieces and insert them nearby.

8 Insert one stem of sedum in the left back corner and let it drape down. Place the second in the same place, but bring it across the front of the basket and glue in place. Cut the third stem in six sections; group three in the right rear corner, and place the rest along the basket front.

9 Insert the feathers into the foam at the front, pointing to the left.

10 Cut the eucalyptus foliage into small pieces, and scatter them throughout the design.

11 Look over the design and make any necessary adjustments.

Faux Fruits

AND VEGETABLES

Faux fruits, vegetables, berries, nuts, and even breads are perfect elements for designs that will be used in a kitchen or dining area. The designs in this group are bright, fresh, and appetizing. The fruits or vegetables are combined with florals that add color and texture. From a rustic cornucopia to strawberries on sparkling "ice," these designs are far from the expected bowl of fruit.

Woodland Cornucopia

FAUX NUTS AND LEAVES

When we see acorns, we immediately know it's fall. In this design, the vines add dimension and a very natural appearance— it looks like the cornucopia has been sitting in the woods and vines have grown around it. If you use this design as a center- piece for Thanksgiving or a fall dinner party, you can extend the theme by tying extra clusters of acorns around the napkins.

Woodland Cornucopia

Florals

Coil of grapevine or honeysuckle vine, 4 to 6 ft. (1.23 to 1.85 m) long

One spray large green foliage

One stem cream/orange lily with two flowers and one bud

Two stems blackberries, 24" (61 cm) long

One stem green hops

One spray of small oak leaves

Three acorn picks with three acorns on each

One stem burnt gold glycerized oak leaves, with ten leaves

Tools and materials

Five 18" (46 cm), 24-gauge wires

Brown floral tape

Wire cutter

4" (10 cm) square green plant foil

Wicker cornucopia, 24" (61 cm) long, with long lip in the front

12" (30.5 cm) square chicken wire

1/3 block dry floral foam

Glue pan and glue

1/2 yd. (0.5 m) copper colored wire-edged ribbon

1   Wrap the wire with floral tape (page 26). Cut two of the wires into fourths. Set aside.

2   Place green plant foil on the bottom of the basket, including the lip. Wrap the foam in chicken wire. Push the wire ends into the foam. Place the foam on the plant foil.

3   Push one end of a long wrapped wire 2" (5 cm) through the wicker on the side of the basket at the edge and twist to secure it. Weave the wire in and out of the chicken wire, secure to the other side of the basket, and push the wire end into the foam. Repeat with the other long wire.

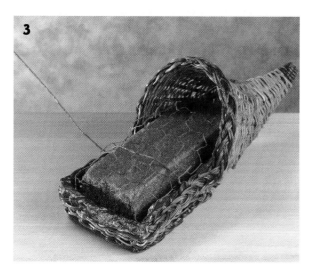

4   Place a coil of grapevine or honeysuckle in and around the cornucopia. Use the short covered wires to secure coils to one another and to the cornucopia; curl the ends of the wire. Add other coils, one at a time. Glue in place.

5   Insert large green leaves in the lower front of the design. Cut the lily into two stems. Insert a lily stem in front of the arrangement so it extends

4

6

8

onto the table. Insert the other lily in the center of the design against the foam.

6 Cut the blackberry stems into two pieces each. Insert the longest blackberry stem at the front close to the lily. Insert the others at random. Remember to keep turning the design as you work so you can see how it will look from all sides.

7 Cut the hops in four pieces. Place them throughout the design for color and texture. Add small oak leaves to cover mechanics.

8 Insert the acorn picks: one near the center lily, one next to the longer lily, one at the back.

9 Cut the oak leaves apart. Glue them here and there in the design to add color.

10 Fold ribbon in half, forming a loop with long tails. Place a long wrapped wire around the loop and twist twice. Insert the wire ends into the foam behind the lilies.

11 Look over the design and make any necessary adjustments.

Market Basket

FAUX VEGETABLES AND BREADS

This is a kitchen design—picture it on an island or dining counter. Choose vegetables your family likes to eat; "picking" them can be a fun outing together. When you make a basket design, people will be less inclined to move your arrangement if you cover the handle with floral materials.

Market Basket

Florals and Vegetables

Assorted faux vegetables such as cauliflower, radishes, carrots, tomatoes, corn, cucumbers; add a bread if you like

Stem of berries and foliage, 24" (61 cm) long

Ivy bush

Tools and materials

Basket with handle, 12" to 24" (30.5 to 61 cm) wide

Dry floral foam

Knife

Green plant foil

Wood picks, wires removed, two for each piece of vegetable or bread

Awl

Glue pan and glue

Two 18" (46 cm), 24-gauge wires

Green floral tape

Wire cutter

1   Insert foam into the basket to 2" (5 cm) below the lip, following the directions on page 24. Secure a small flat chunk of foam to the center for added height.

2   Arrange the faux foods in the basket without attaching them yet. Once you know which side will face down, make two closely spaced, small holes in each one with an awl. Glue a wood pick into each hole. Insert each piece into the foam.

3   Wrap the wire with the floral tape (page 26). Cut each piece into quarters. Curve the berry stem along the edge and handle of the basket and secure it with the wrapped wire.

4   Cut the ivy bush into long, medium, and short pieces. Glue them in the foam at the bottom of the handle on one side. Wrap some around the handle and some around the edge of the basket. Glue other pieces to cover any exposed foam or gaps between the vegetables.

5   Look over the design and make any necessary adjustments.

Strawberries on Ice

FRESH, COOL, GARDEN-PICKED

In this appealing presentation, elegant, red roses nestle over fresh, ripe strawberries on a cool bed of faux ice. Place the "chilly" bowl where it can be viewed from just below eye level, as it is sure to attract looks and temperature-testing touches from curious admirers.

Strawberries on Ice

Florals

Eight to 12 artificial strawberries

Three open roses with foliage

Two branches with strawberries, blossoms, and foliage

Tools and materials

Round glass bowl, 10" (25.5 cm) in diameter

White distilled vinegar; paper towel

Duct tape

Anchor pin

Glue pan and glue

3" (7.5 cm) block white Styrofoam

Plastic ice crystals, 1 pound bag

1   Wash the container. Dip a paper towel in vinegar; wipe the inside of the bowl base, and allow it to dry.

2   Place a piece of duct tape, 2" (5 cm) long, in the middle, bottom of the bowl. Dip the flat side of the anchor pin in the glue pan; glue it onto the duct tape with the prongs up.

3   Secure the Styrofoam on top of the prongs.

4   Add artificial ice crystals to the bowl around and over the foam.

5   Place the strawberries around the top of the ice.

6   Remove the foliage from the rose stems. Cut the rose stems to 5" (12.7 cm); place them deep into the foam so the outer petals rest under the lip of the bowl.

7 Cut the berry branches into four parts each. Insert the stems into the foam to cover it.

8 Look over the design and make any necessary adjustments.

Not Just a Fruit Bowl

FRUITS WITH FLOWERS

Faux fruits make colorful centerpieces. In a typical fruit bowl, though, many of the fruits are hidden. In this design, fruits are displayed in a mound. The effect is colorful and abundant—as fruit should look. The orbiting flowers are Gloriosa lilies.

Not Just a Fruit Bowl

Fruits and Florals

Three clusters large grapes

Two clusters champagne grapes

Assorted fruits, such as apples, lemons, limes, peaches, pears, pomegranates, and oranges

Three stems variegated ivy

Two stems poppies, one cut slightly shorter than the other

Three stems Gloriosa lilies, each with three flowers

Ten strawberries

Tools and materials

Large stone container that looks like a compote

Dry floral foam

Knife

Glue pan and glue

22 wood picks, each 6" (15 cm) long, with wire removed from 15

Awl

Wire cutter

1 Cut the foam so it will fill the container completely from side to side and sit just above the lip. Secure it into the container.

2 Cut a second piece of foam, 3" (7.5 cm) square. Insert wood picks in the center of the foam in the container. Dab them with glue and press the second piece of foam on top, securing it.

3 Wrap the stem of each grape cluster tightly with the wire of a wood pick. Insert the pick on a large grape cluster into the foam at the lip of the container and let it hang over the edge. Insert the second and third clusters a bit higher and drape them over the edge. Turn the container around and insert the champagne grape clusters together near the edge, draping down.

4 Arrange the faux foods (except the strawberries) without attaching them yet. As you place each fruit, work for a balance of colors, sizes, and textures. Keep turning the design as you work. Show off the most interesting feature of each fruit—the stem end of the apple, the shape of the pear from the side, the navel of the orange. Once you know which side will face down, make two small holes in each piece with an awl. Glue a wood pick into each hole. Insert each piece into the foam, pointing each pick toward the center of the foam base.

5 Cut clusters of leaves from the ivy stems. Glue them under and between fruits.

6 Insert the shorter poppy at the bottom of the foam to the side. Insert the longer poppy a few inches higher. Turn their faces up to the sun.

7 Cut the lilies into pieces, leaving one flower on each stem. Insert the stems of the lilies throughout the arrangement and bend the stems gracefully.

8 Touch the strawberries into the glue in the pan and place them wherever you need some color or texture or where you need to conceal foam. Use leftover ivy leaves to cover any foam that still shows.

9 Look over the design and make any necessary adjustments.

Kitchen Brightener

WRAPPED CONTAINERS

Transform an inexpensive
container by wrapping it with
large leaves, ribbon, or fabric.
This cheerful, slightly funky
design for a kitchen or casual
dining area uses cabbage leaves.
Measure the leaves, then choose
a container that will be covered
completely, with the leaves
extending slightly over the top.

Kitchen Brightener

Florals

Pre-rolled cabbage with six leaves

Six gerberas

Tools and materials

Inexpensive container

Double-sided tape

Large rubber band

Three strands colored raffia

1 Wrap double-sided tape around the container at the top and 3" (7.5 cm) from the bottom.

2 Lay the cabbage roll on your work surface. Position the container on top and wrap the roll around it with one end overlapping the other. Put the rubber band around the middle of the container to hold the cabbage in place.

3 Cover the rubber band with a double wrap of raffia. Tie with a bow and let the ends pool on the table.

4 Place the gerberas in the center of the design with the heads resting on top of the leaves.

5 Look over the design and make any necessary adjustments.

Index